"Cunningham brings Dewey's naturalism in conversation with insights from systems theory in order to raise some probing questions about contemporary schooling. Clear, accessible, eloquent and passionate."—Gert Biesta, Professor of Educational Theory and Policy, University of Luxembourg, Luxembourg, and author of *The Beautiful Risk of Education* (2014)

"A breath of fresh air in an era of stale schooling! Cunningham gives us valuable suggestions to build on diversity, professional choice, interdisciplinary collaboration, and—yes—joy in education."—Nel Noddings, Lee Jacks Professor of Education Emerita, Stanford University, USA, and author of *Education and Democracy in the 21st Century* (2013)

DOI: 10.1057/9781137449320.0001

The Cultural and Social Foundations of Education

Series Editor: **A.G. Rud**, Distinguished Professor in the College of Education of Washington State University, USA.

The Palgrave Pivot series on the Cultural and Social Foundations of Education seeks to understand educational practices around the world through the interpretive lenses provided by the disciplines of philosophy, history, sociology, politics, and cultural studies. This series focuses on the following major themes: **democracy and social justice, ethics, sustainability education, technology, and the imagination.** It publishes the best current thinking on those topics, as well as reconsideration of historical figures and major thinkers in education.

Titles include:

Craig A. Cunningham
SYSTEMS THEORY FOR PRAGMATIC SCHOOLING
Toward Principles of Democratic Education

Aaron Stoller
KNOWING AND LEARNING AS CREATIVE ACTION
A Reexamination of the Epistemological Foundations of Education

Sue Ellen Henry
CHILDREN'S BODIES IN SCHOOLS
Corporeal Performances of Social Class

Clarence W. Joldersma
A LEVINASIAN ETHICS FOR EDUCATION'S COMMONPLACES
Between Calling and Inspiration

DOI: 10.1057/9781137449320.0001

palgrave▸pivot

Systems Theory for Pragmatic Schooling: Toward Principles of Democratic Education

Craig A. Cunningham

Associate Professor, National College of Education, National Louis University, Chicago, USA

DOI: 10.1057/9781137449320.0001

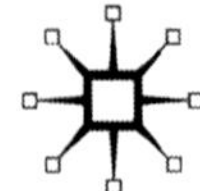

SYSTEMS THEORY FOR PRAGMATIC SCHOOLING

First published in 2014 by
PALGRAVE MACMILLAN®
in the United States—a division of St. Martin's Press LLC,
175 Fifth Avenue, New York, NY 10010.

Where this book is distributed in the UK, Europe and the rest of the world, this is by Palgrave Macmillan, a division of Macmillan Publishers Limited, registered in England, company number 785998, of Houndmills, Basingstoke, Hampshire RG21 6XS.

Palgrave Macmillan is the global academic imprint of the above companies and has companies and representatives throughout the world.

ISBN: 978-1-137-44933-7 EPUB
ISBN: 978-1-137-44932-0 PDF
ISBN: 978-1-137-44931-3 Hardback

Library of Congress Cataloging-in-Publication Data is available from the Library of Congress.

A catalogue record of the book is available from the British Library.

First edition: 2014

www.palgrave.com/pivot

DOI: 10.1057/9781137449320

The aim of science is to seek the simplest explanations of complex facts.

We are apt to fall into the error of thinking that the facts are simple because simplicity is the goal of our quest. The guiding motto in the life of every natural philosopher should be,

"Seek simplicity and distrust it."

—Alfred North Whitehead,
The Concept of Nature (1920)

DOI: 10.1057/9781137449320.0001

This book is dedicated to Rowan and Thomas. Your differences and complexities never fail to amaze and inspire.

DOI: 10.1057/9781137449320.0001

Contents

DOI: 10.1057/9781137449320.0001

Series Editor's Preface

The Palgrave Pivot series *Cultural and Social Foundations of Education* seeks to understand educational practices around the world through the interpretive lenses provided by the disciplines of philosophy, history, sociology, politics, and cultural studies. This series focuses on the following major themes: democracy and social justice, ethics, sustainability education, technology, and the imagination. It publishes the best current thinking on those topics, as well as reconsiderations of historical figures and major thinkers in education.

The cultural and social foundations of education are enjoying a rebirth. While studies of Plato, Pestalozzi, and Dewey or analyses of the effects of Supreme Court decisions or world economic policies have always been important to understand education, there is increased urgency for such work in today's educational climate. Education is seen in both the developed and developing world as a means to social advancement and improvement of life. More than ever there are questions about what kind of education should be provided and for whom. In addition, information technologies are rapidly transforming teaching and learning, while a political climate in many countries emphasizes market solutions to social problems at the same time that it moves away from democratic forms of schooling.

Out of this rich context, the *Cultural and Social Foundations of Education* series was established to explore five themes important in schooling in short books by leading and rising scholars. I chose themes that are of perennial

DOI: 10.1057/9781137449320.0002

importance to the foundations of education, such as democracy and social justice, as well as newer emphases, such as technology and sustainability that scholars are exploring. Democracy and social justice has been a perennial theme in foundations of education, and continues to have greater urgency. This series will feature works that examine worldwide issues related to democracy and social justice, from the effects of wealth and income inequality on schools in developed countries to the spread of democracy and social justice concerns to other countries around the world. Closely related to this is the second theme of ethics: issues of right, wrong, fairness, equity, and equality in schools and educational practices worldwide. Increased attention is being paid to our planet's health, so how we can educate our children to accept and deal with environmental degradation forms the third theme. What it means to educate for a sustainable future is a question that foundation scholars are increasingly addressing. For a fourth theme, the impact of information technology upon education is enormous and not something that should be left just to technical experts in that area. There is a need for scholars in the cultural and social foundations of education to inquire critically about the claims made by technology and to inform us about new developments in this area. Finally, the arts and imagination are all too often pushed to the margins of schooling especially today, and so this topic forms the fifth theme. Scholars of foundations have long championed the importance of this area: in the past century, John Dewey made a compelling argument for the importance of art and the imagination and especially for supporting the arts in educational practice in his late work, *Art as Experience*.

The volumes in the series will be both single authored and edited collections, and serve as accessible resources for those interested in foundational issues in education at all levels, particularly advanced undergraduate and graduate students in education and the social sciences who are being exposed to the latest thinking on issues of perennial importance and relevance to the context and practices of education worldwide.

A. G. Rud

DOI: 10.1057/9781137449320.0002

About the Author

Craig A. Cunningham, Ph.D., is Associate Professor at National Louis University in Chicago, where he teaches courses and does research in the history and philosophy of education, technology in education, urban teaching, policy, and research. Craig has been a high school teacher, school administrator, chair of his college faculty, and has designed and directed teacher professional development programs. Craig is the proud father of Rowan and Thomas.

DOI: 10.1057/9781137449320.0003

Acknowledgments

For helping me get my mind around some of the issues in this book, I thank Philip W. Jackson, Chip Bruce, Debbie Seltzer-Kelly, Jim Garrison, Leonard Waks, Nora Bateson, and Richard Quantz.

For wide-ranging conversations I thank Sharon Comstock, Julia Brazas, Gale Stam, Tamar Friedman, Janet Gray-McKennis, Amy Shuffelton, Sean York, and Ed Cunningham.

I thank Pat Ashley for her detailed and extremely helpful comments on the manuscript, Sarah Nathan and A.G. Rud for their sustained enthusiasm throughout the project, and Mara Berkoff for her cheery and tireless support.

I thank my Facebook homies for responding to various trial balloons, especially Jonathon Richter, Heidi Nordberg, Sam Guido, Maya Levanon, Mark Byrnes, Stephen Thompson, Stephen Cohen, Mark Larson, Pennie Lundquist, Darby Charvat, Brian Burtt, Irish Bain, Nicole Zumpano, David Spearman, and Connie Weber.

I thank the Leadership Cabinet of the National College of Education for the opportunity to participate in extensive discussions about the complexities of education. I especially thank Alison Hilsabeck, who was an exceptional dean and is a fine interlocutor and a nurturing friend.

I want to thank my students over the past few years, who have helped me to clarify what I was trying to say about systems, modeling, and complexity.

Finally, I thank Joseph W. Gauld, the founder of the Hyde School in Bath, Maine, who taught me the importance of character and unique potential.

Introduction

Abstract: *American democracy is in crisis partly because American schools are not adequately preparing students—and society—for dealing with the complex challenges of the future. The problem is primarily conceptual; we need new ways of thinking about schooling. We need to shift from the attempt to standardize our students and instead focus on celebrating and supporting diversity.*

Cunningham, Craig A. *Systems Theory for Pragmatic Schooling: Toward Principles of Democratic Education.* New York: Palgrave Macmillan, 2014.
DOI: 10.1057/9781137449320.0005.

I am worried about the future of American democracy.

You should be, too. Why?

I see an increasing bifurcation of the American population into two distinct political camps that represent two very different cultures.

I also see a breakdown in the public consensus about the purposes of public schools.

I see an alarming increase in corporate power in determining educational policy and profiting from public schooling. Some of these corporations—and the "school reform" efforts they fund—are wantonly disregarding the traditions and ideals of public schooling, ignoring the common-sense notion that the quality of the commons—the public space that we all share—represents something that we should nurture and sustain.

I see ongoing threats to the separation of church and state, with continuing efforts by American religious fundamentalists to take control of certain aspects of the school curriculum, imposing their values into the public schools. I see other fundamentalists worldwide who have learned to hate and fear the United States and its way of life, and who seek to destroy it.

I see many complaints about the "soullessness" of American public schools, even by liberals and humanists. This suggests that we have succeeded in "demystifying" schooling (Bowers, 1985), but have failed to replace traditional religious concepts with more appropriate ideals. We need new ways of talking about the sacred potential of each person, and a new emphasis on fostering joy in schools rather than the dehumanizing drudgery of compliance.

I see a growing gap between the poor and the rich, and the multiple effects that this disparity has on motivation, the allocation of public and private debt, and on central social problems such as crime, depression, and alcoholism. An enormous gap between the poor and the rich has negative effects on the rich as well as the poor (Wilkinson & Pickett, 2010). This suggests that we all need to work together to reduce this inequality.

I see an American public that is increasingly distrustful of those who are well educated and astonishingly ignorant of history, statistics, and the findings of modern science. How can we expect the typical American to participate in discussions about the future of our society if they don't understand the centrality of evolution to the advancement of the biological sciences, the significance of relativity and quantum theory to

DOI: 10.1057/9781137449320.0005

what is real and to what we can know, and the ways that modeling and data are used in understanding complex phenomena such as climate change (Jacoby, 2008; Pallant, Lee & Pryputniewicz, 2012), and if they distrust those who know a lot about these topics? This ignorance has the potential to destroy our democracy.

I see many students who are studying to be teachers—and many people who are *already* teachers—stuck like other Americans in the ideas of the 18th century, lacking a fundamental understanding of the challenges of *complexity* in a rapidly changing world (Gough, 1989; Mashhadi & Woolnough, 1999).[1]

Yes, I said *18th century.*

Many of these problems are either a result of the failures of schooling or are exacerbated by the failures of schooling. Many of our schools are not up-to-date with knowledge and ideas from the 19th or 20th centuries, especially in science but across multiple areas of the curriculum. That is simply not good enough for the schooling of kids born in the 21st century.

Some American schools do a very good job of preparing their students to think critically about complex problems from a variety of perspectives. These tend to be schools that serve the children of the wealthy or highly selective schools that admit small percentages of those who apply. Schools that admit all students, however, especially those whose population comes primarily from low income families, generally do a very poor job of preparing their students for the higher level thinking and the highly skilled jobs likely to be in demand as they reach adulthood.

Let me put this bluntly. *American schools—for the most part—are failing to prepare American society for the future.*

We actually *don't know* what our children will face in the future, although we can be certain that things are going to get more challenging. Because we don't know for sure, we need to educate today's students to be ready for an array of complex problems, which means giving them broad skills in inquiry, critical thinking, and flexibility. We also need to think about what we want for the society as a whole, and the ways that schools are preparing our society for the future.

The necessary shift is in part conceptual. We need new ways to *think* about schooling. It is a matter of how we think affecting what we do. It's rooted in the systemic patterns of our understanding (Bateson, 2011).

DOI: 10.1057/9781137449320.0005

Most importantly, we need to recognize that the diversity of the American people is our biggest strength. *Standardization doesn't work!*

We need a better appreciation of the complexity of schooling and of the many smaller systems involved in schooling. We need a better understanding of the value of diversity and variation in those systems.

As Whitehead says in the epigraph to this book, science seeks simplicity, *but we should distrust it.*

We need to shift schooling from trying to match diverse students to acceptable standards and instead focus on developing the unique potential of diverse human beings. *This will require revolutionary change.*

I offer this book as "philosophical midwifery" (Kitcher, 2011, p. 253) to help this new way of thinking to emerge. I will combine the pragmatic naturalism of John Dewey with contemporary systems theory to reconceive schooling. The primary goal is to convince you that schooling is about *fostering* diversity, *not* about getting diverse individuals to conform to predefined standards.[2]

Notes

1 A simple definition of **complexity** is "changeability, variability; having a lot of different states or modes, or doing a lot of different things. Something is simple when it is all the same" (Godfrey-Smith, 1998, p. 24).

2 In order to capture the complexity of schooling and of the ideas in this book, I have built a comprehensive Index, which includes numerous cross-cutting concepts. I recommend that you use the Index to access these concepts in a non-linear way, particularly after reading through the book once.

DOI: 10.1057/9781137449320.0005

1
The Schooling We Have

Abstract: *American schools are organized like factories, which doesn't work well, partly because humans are not interchangeable parts. Educational policy-makers use a rhetoric of crisis to impose simplistic solutions that fail to address central issues. Instead of asking what schools are really for, we offer a vague and incoherent curriculum that reduces everything to isolated bits of knowledge and fails to give students a sense of the big picture. A combination of John Dewey's pragmatic naturalism and systems theory can offer an alternative conception.*

Cunningham, Craig A. *Systems Theory for Pragmatic Schooling: Toward Principles of Democratic Education.* New York: Palgrave Macmillan, 2014.
DOI: 10.1057/9781137449320.0006.

American schooling is in transition.

It is hard to see the significance of this change, because we are in the middle of it. If we could jump ten or twenty years into the future, we would see the change. Let's hope we would see what we want to see!

Changing our schooling is sorely needed. The typical American school reflects organizational and management decisions made more than a hundred years ago, when the world was in the Industrial Age. The reigning metaphors then were the *machine*, and the combination of machines in *factories*.

Our schools resemble a collection of *machines* in *factories* more than they resemble anything else.

Students are organized into grades by their age, in roughly identical classrooms, with a single teacher in each classroom, teaching predetermined curricula divided up into subject and grade levels, using teacher-centered learning activities that require student compliance, with periodic quizzes and tests serving as quality control (Waks, 2014). Students are fed into one end of the system as small children, and they proceed in lock-step through the grades, receiving the same treatments along the way, acquiring bits of chopped-up knowledge and skill at each stage, and emerging at the other end. This basic and simplistic structure varies very little (Davis & Sumara, 2000).

What's more, the primary thing students *learn* in schools is "habituation to the norms of industrial life rather than academic learning" (Waks, 2014, p. 40). Students learn to do what they are told, learn what they are supposed to learn, submit to standard forms of assessment and accept the judgments applied, and treat each other according to their roles within the institution rather than as whole human beings. I don't quite get why this is what we want of our kids.

The world has moved beyond the Industrial Age and factory schools don't work very well in the new age. For one thing, humans aren't interchangeable parts. They don't always comply with what's expected. Factory schools ignore the facts "that learning must be active and that children learn in different ways and at different rates" (Abbott & McTaggart, 2010, p. 197).

Leonard Waks (2014) points to other failures. Factory schools "fail to promote academic achievement and the desired graduation rate"; they are "wasteful of the energies and capabilities of students and teachers"; they "fail to connect young people to worlds of opportunity"; and they

DOI: 10.1057/9781137449320.0006

"are losing their legitimacy as their failures lead citizens to withdraw their support" (p. 189).

I would add that too much emphasis is placed on the individual student, on competition, on grades, on sorting students by academic ability, and on meeting pre-specified expectations rather than helping students to think creatively and originally (Robinson, 2011).

The educational policy environment is not especially helpful. "Fixes" are legitimated through a discourse of "crisis": most commonly in recent years the so-called crisis of global economic competitiveness (Bartos, 2012; Lauder et al., 2012; Nordin, 2014). The alarmism is striking. When international comparison test results were released in 2010, Arne Duncan, the US Secretary of Education, said they were a "wake-up call" (Barboza, 2010). Wake-up call? I have to think that this discourse is intended to undermine support for public schooling in the United States, suggesting that *nothing* we've been doing is right. This is hard to accept. But this way of talking isn't new: it's been around at least since *A Nation at Risk* (United States, 1983). Politicians want the American public to think that public schools are terrible. Why is that?

The crisis discourse, once it becomes widespread, becomes a kind of common sense assumption that is hard to contradict or dislodge, even with good evidence. The problem with the crisis mentality is that it tries to "fix" the perceived problem or problems without considering whether the system as a whole needs to be *transformed* or whether maybe we're thinking about the whole thing in the wrong way. It uses simplistic measures of success, based on simplified understandings of the needs of the past, to force changes that center specifically on those simplified measures. What's more, the attempted "fixes" are generally piecemeal, focusing on just one part rather than the system as a whole.

Responding to the crisis becomes the preoccupation of policy makers and the public, thus sidelining the need to reconsider "What are our schools for?"

I argue that the "crisis" is not so much a crisis of *schooling* as a crisis of *perception*.

We need to change the way we *see* things.

Instead of running schools as factories, with a reductionist, mechanical mindset that doles out knowledge and skills bit by bit and aims for standardization, we need to emphasize complexity and the interrelationships of things from the *beginning* (yes, even with young kids) and encourage

DOI: 10.1057/9781137449320.0006

diverse perspectives and out-of-the-box thinking.[1] Each child's uniqueness is a *strength*, and our schools need to be redesigned to celebrate and nurture those qualities. We need to reconceive of the people involved in schools—students, teachers, administrators, parents— as well as the schools themselves in terms of relationships and context rather than in isolation.

We should aim for engagement, joy, deep learning, critical awareness, understanding of systems and complexity, and belief in the value of democratic discourse. Our public schools need to take a stand in *favor* of democratic approaches to solving social problems, not aim at neutrality with regard to the importance of sustaining public discourse. Our public schools should be *for* a flourishing public.

The curriculum we have

The curriculum in American schools tends to be "vague" and "incoherent" (Hirsch, 2006, p. 317). What is learned in school varies considerably from state to state. Because teachers often get to decide what content is emphasized, the curriculum also varies quite a bit from classroom to classroom. And since the *amount* of content in the curriculum keeps increasing over time, teachers spend less and less time on important concepts. It's not possible to teach everything.

Partly because of the ways schools and teachers are evaluated, but also because of a simplistic view of learning, schools tend to focus on dispensing and assessing "discrete bits of information" (Boyles, 2006, p. 67). "Coverage" of the curriculum is the priority (Gardner, 2007). Teachers try to "get through" the materials in their textbooks or curriculum guides, and students are prepared to regurgitate this rapidly digested information in papers and examinations. The overall effect is a kind of mind-numbing social reproduction. Kids from wealthier families are prepared for high-level jobs and kids from lower-income families are prepared for low-level jobs (Anyon, 1997).

What's worse, our schools seem to be pushing a "curriculum for consumption":

> The harder you work, children have been told, and the more exams you pass, the better job you will get, the more money you will earn; with that will come a bigger car, larger house, more wine and fine clothes, and holidays taken regularly on the other side of the globe. (Abbott & McTaggart, 2010, p. 193)

DOI: 10.1057/9781137449320.0006

The purpose seems to be to increase compliance and conformity—and to prepare young people to plug themselves into the economic order so they can earn and spend money—rather than to increase their adaptability for a changing world or help them think about the big challenges that our world faces in the 21st century.

Why do we have this kind of curriculum?

Lawrence Cremin (1990), the great historian of American education, makes it plain:

> Out of a process that involves all three branches of government at the state and federal levels as well as thousands of local school boards, a plethora of private interests ranging from publishers to accrediting agencies, and the variety of professionals who actually operate the schools emerges what we call the curriculum, with its requirements, its electives, its informal activities, and its unacknowledged routines. It is that curriculum, in various versions, that is supposed to be offered to all the children of all the people. (p. 36)

Curriculum is often set by third parties, rather than by the members of a school community (Murgatroyd, 2010). This reduces autonomy and tends to define the teacher as the "deliverer" of a curriculum instead of as a key stakeholder. The curriculum that results reflects the values of those involved in its development, but not in a particularly well-thought-out way. If the mainstream textbooks that most schools use are any indication, the curriculum is more like a grab bag of random isolated facts and disconnected skills, assembled with attention to marketing to test-anxious administrators and harried teachers, rather than presenting a coherent picture of our complex world.

Thinking about schooling

The title of this book refers to "schooling," because I am going to draw attention to *general* features of schooling that apply regardless of the school—even to schooling that takes place *outside* schools (such as homeschooling).

We need to distinguish schooling from **education**, which is a much broader term that covers all of the ways that people become who they are.[2] **Schooling** refers to the *intentional* process of organizing the activi-

DOI: 10.1057/9781137449320.0006

ties of learners to produce learning. An education can be gotten by accident and is often absorbed from the larger culture, whereas schooling is organized, typically in institutions. Schooling involves a coordination of multiple efforts; it is systematic and systematized (Vanderstraeten, 2000).

Training is a specific type of schooling that involves an organized, intentional effort to produce specific and *predictable* outcomes. Not all training occurs in schools: much of it takes place in the workplace. But a lot of what goes on in schools is better described as training than as education. Indeed, we could say that the purpose of schooling historically has been to shape learners so that they conform to social expectations, which is inherently a *training* function rather than an *education* function.

Socialization is another form of training, although its purposes tend to be more general and it takes place as much in families as in schools. Historically, systems of schooling emerge when society becomes too complex for adequate socialization to occur in families. Put differently, societies build systems of schooling when typical parents are no longer able to train their children for the demands of the larger society.

To understand schooling in a given society, we need to understand how it relates to the larger society. To simplify, we can look at the society's political economy and ideology. **Political economy** is the way that the society is structured, in terms of making a living, daily routines, population distribution, and voting. **Ideology**, on the other hand, is the assumptions that people make that shape their thinking across multiple domains.

Picture an equilateral triangle, with schooling at one corner, ideology at another, and political economy at the third. Each of the sides of the triangle has arrows at both ends, indicating that the influence goes in both directions. So ideology affects schooling, and schooling affects ideology. Political economy affects schooling, and schooling affects political economy. Finally, political economy affects ideology, and ideology affects political economy (Tozer, Senese, & Violas, 2013). This analytical framework gives us a simple model of how schools and societies are related. Models are one of the most useful ways of understanding complex systems, as we'll see.

Let's focus specifically on the corner of the triangle labeled "ideology," which we can think of as the "controlling system of ideas" in a society (Hirsch, 1996, p. 15). How does American ideology impact American schooling?

DOI: 10.1057/9781137449320.0006

To answer that question, we need to understand our *own* thinking. That's not always easy. Ideologies are often implicit and not clearly articulated. For example, many contemporary teachers and school administrators use a simplistic behaviorist conception of learning that was widespread in the 19th and 20th centuries. For this reason, some people involved in schooling may not grasp the true complexity of learning. There are other components of ideology that affect schooling, many of which we will explore in this book. Along the way, you will learn some new ways of thinking. For these to be useful, your beliefs or mental maps may have to change, or at least open up to new understandings.

Most of the readers of this book learned **analysis** at school—how to break things into their constituent parts, to understand the world from the perspective of a particular subject, or to look for exactly what is causing a particular problem. Schools are better at teaching this than they are at teaching **synthesis**, which is a process of putting things together in ways that generate deeper understanding. Schools tend to teach us how to understand *aspects* of complex situations—abstracted out of their complexities—but not so much whole situations.

As John Dewey, whom many of the readers of this book know from his educational ideas, wrote:

> Modern preoccupation with science and with industry based on science has been disastrous: our education has followed the model that they have set. It has been concerned with intellectual analysis and formularized information.... [This]...is disastrous because it has fixed attention upon competition for control and possession of a fixed environment rather than...[creating] an environment. It is disastrous because civilization built upon these principles cannot supply the demand of the soul for joy, or freshness of experience. ("Art in Education—and Education in Art," 1926, LW 2.112)[3]

Analysis has its applications, particularly in understanding cause and effect (Siegrist et al., 2013). The emphasis on analysis also works well for preparing people for specific disciplines, or to be specialists (Abbott & McTaggart, 2010). Unfortunately, it also causes us to ignore complexity (Hacker, 1994) and fails to promote deeper learning, "the process through which an individual becomes capable of taking what was learned in one situation and applying it to a new situation" (Pellegrino & Hilton, 2012). Another type of thinking that is often ignored in schools is **evaluative thinking**: the assignment of value to different possibilities.

If our society is going to successfully confront some of the problems facing us in this century, we're going to have to change the way we teach

DOI: 10.1057/9781137449320.0006

the next generation. We are going to have to teach our children to understand complexity and to apply that understanding to the big issues that the world faces (Galinsky, 2010; Pellegrino & Hilton, 2012). Thinking about complex problems requires a more sophisticated understanding of the nature of reality (Mitchell, 2009). This requires a shift in our own conceptions of the nature of nature.

Pragmatic naturalism

Dewey examined the nature of reality throughout his long career. His explicitly educational books—the ones most likely to have been read by educators, including *School and Society* (1899), *Democracy and Education* (1916), and *Experience and Education* (1938)—say a lot that is relevant today to schooling, but these books tend to ignore some deeper philosophical issues.

In *Democracy and Education,* Dewey hints at the importance of understanding nature.

> "Nature" is indeed a vague and metaphorical term, but one thing that "Nature" may be said to utter is that there are conditions of educational efficiency, and that till we have learned what these conditions are and have learned to make our practices accord with them, the noblest and most ideal of our aims are doomed to suffer—are verbal and sentimental rather than efficacious. (MW 9.122)

When Dewey wrote these words, he had not yet developed an adequate understanding of the "qualities and relations of the world in which our action goes on, [and the] factors upon which the accomplishment of our purposes depends" (MW 9.141) to supply the principles of schooling that he sought. This is one reason he spent the next 35 years looking at deeper philosophical issues, such as the nature of experience, how humans inquire and learn and grow, and what he referred to as the "generic traits of existence." In several of his later non-educational books, especially *Experience and Nature* (1925) and *Art as Experience* (1934), Dewey developed an understanding of the nature of nature that offers profound guidance for schooling. But he never fully explicated the educational implications of these ideas, partly because he remained unsatisfied with his conceptions up until the end of his life (Jackson, 2002).

Dewey remained unsatisfied with his conception of the nature of nature, I believe, because he lacked an understanding of the importance

DOI: 10.1057/9781137449320.0006

of systems and complexity. Systems theory and complexity science did not emerge until after his death. But from our perspective, we can see how these developments extend Dewey's thinking and fulfill Dewey's vision for how an understanding of nature can inform schooling.

Dewey's overall system of ideas can be referred to as "pragmatic naturalism." I will argue that Dewey's concept of "situation" is the intellectual precursor to the development of systems theory. Exploring the compatibilities and synergies between Dewey's pragmatic naturalism and systems theory—and the application of a synthesized perspective to schooling—is a central goal of this book.

Systems theory

The great discovery of the 20th century is that we do not encounter things in the world as isolated, singular, or disconnected. *All* things *come embedded in situations*, most involving multiple entities in interaction. Multiple entities in interaction can be understood as systems. "Every person we encounter, every organization, every animal, garden, tree, and forest is a complex system" (Meadows & Wright, 2008, p. 3). Each of these systems involves multiple interrelationships within itself and with its environment.

I think most readers of this book have general sense of what a system is. Most of us are familiar with computer systems, transportation systems, nervous systems, and the solar system. Some of us may even have a sense of what "*The System*" is!

Meadows and Wright (2008) give a simple definition: "A **system** is a set of things—people, cells, molecules, or whatever—interconnected in such a way that they produce their own pattern of behavior over time" (p. 2). There are some similarities in the ways that different kinds of systems behave across multiple domains, so we can make some generalizations. This is a form of analogic reasoning, and it is fundamental to thinking in general, but especially to thinking *about the general* or about what is true of everything, especially systems. The study of the similarities of different kinds of systems can be referred to as "systems theory."

It turns out that it is possible to see *everything that exists* in terms of a systems lens or framework. This helps us to see things in their complexities and interrelationships. Combined with the understandings of the nature of nature provided by pragmatic naturalism, systems theory

DOI: 10.1057/9781137449320.0006

offers us a unified understanding of the nature of reality—a view that can help inform a new conception of schooling. These two perspectives are surprisingly compatible. Both, for example, offer support for pluralism and democracy.

Before we talk specifically about schooling, we need to lay the groundwork for a synthesis of pragmatic naturalism and systems theory. That is the focus of the next two chapters.

Notes

1 An excellent source of learning materials related to systems thinking at all ages is http://watersfoundation.org/.
2 My distinctions among schooling, education, and training are adapted from those described in Tozer, Senese, and Violas (2013).
3 All John Dewey references in this book are to the *Collected Works* (published by Southern Illinois University Press) and are given in the form LW 2.112, where the first two letters refer to whether the work is in the Early Works, Middle Works, or Later Works; the first number refers to the volume in that series; and the number after the period refers to the page number of that volume.

DOI: 10.1057/9781137449320.0006

2
The Nature of Nature

Abstract: *John Dewey's philosophy of experience offers a view of the nature of nature than can help us to reconceive schooling. Dewey offers us a set of the generic traits of existences, including interaction, temporality, complexity, and qualitative uniqueness. When we experience doubt or uncertainty, we examine distinctions and relations as part of inquiry, which is how we deal with environmental complexity. We acquire habits, including knowledge and meaning, through the use of intelligence and imagination in the attempt to secure desired goods. An example of social inquiry is given and discussed, with an emphasis on the difference between standards and criteria.*

Cunningham, Craig A. *Systems Theory for Pragmatic Schooling: Toward Principles of Democratic Education.* New York: Palgrave Macmillan, 2014.
DOI: 10.1057/9781137449320.0007.

Gregory Bateson, who understood nature better than almost anyone, said:

> The major problems of the world are the result of the difference between how nature works and the way people think. (Bateson, 2011)

Let's take this comment seriously. What are those differences? How does nature work? Most importantly, what can we say about the way nature works that is relevant to understanding problems related to schooling in the 21st century?

Philosophy can seem remote from such relevance. Dewey referred to the typical topics of philosophical examination as "the problems of philosophers" and distinguished them from "the problems of men." The problems of philosophers concern such things as how we know what we know ("**epistemology**"), the nature of being ("**metaphysics**"), the nature of the good ("**ethics**"), and what beauty is ("**aesthetics**"). We all have beliefs about these issues, but most of us don't abstract them from daily life. Philosophers do.

The purpose of philosophical excursions away from daily life—at least according to Dewey—is to come back into the everyday and use the understandings gained through philosophy as tools for clarifying and achieving our real-world goals. This strong connection between thought and action is one of the reasons that Dewey's point of view is called *pragmatism*. "The real sign of a vibrant philosophy," writes Boisvert (1998a), "is its fruitfulness in guiding us toward enhanced human lives" (p. 27).[1] I want to realize this vision in understanding schooling.

Dewey's examination into the nature of nature occurred at a time when people across the sciences, social sciences, and the humanities were also rethinking their general understandings of the nature of reality. Dewey's ideas were influenced by these changes—most importantly, a shift from seeing nature as a machine made up of basic building blocks to understanding it as a network of interrelationships (Capra & Luisi, 2014). Dewey understood the times in which he wrote:

> The question of whether we should begin with the simple or the complex appears to me the most important problem in philosophic method at the present time. (Dewey, "The Inclusive Philosophic Idea," 1928, LW 3.42)

Dewey's own preference was to pay close attention to complexities.

DOI: 10.1057/9781137449320.0007

Experience

Reality, for Dewey, is completely *natural*. There is nothing *supernatural* or *transcendent*, in his view. That is why we refer to his views as a form of *naturalism* (Ryder, 2013; Schulkin, 2012).

Nature doesn't come to us all at once: we can't know it all at once. Instead, we are born into a world that, at least initially, is a "blooming, buzzing confusion" as William James (1890, p. 462) put it. It takes time for us to transform this confusion into a coherent world view. To do that, we need *experience*. Experience is our interface to reality: we know reality through it.

For Dewey, experience is pretty much everything—or at least our primary guide to understanding everything. Experience is the combination of what we *do*, and what we *undergo*. This is important. We don't just experience the world passively. It doesn't just "come to us" as we sit and reflect on what it means. We *act*. It is *through* our actions that we come to understand the world.

In a famous article early in his career, "The Reflex Arc Concept in Psychology" (1896), Dewey uses the example of a child's first experience with a candle. The child may, in conjunction with seeing the candle, reach out to touch the flame, "burning" with desire to figure out what it is. This is a universal human impulse. If the child puts her finger into the flame, she will suddenly feel pain and quickly withdraw her hand. Fortunately, for her, this is a reflex, hard-wired by evolution. The child may look more intently at the flame, but now avoid touching it. It has a new meaning for her. Maybe she will poke at it with a nearby toy. Why? *To see what happens*. This is what humans do to understand their world: they poke and prod. At this point, an older person nearby may take the flame away or put it out. But the child has had an experience. The *doing* (initially seeing and being captivated by the flame, reaching out to touch it, poking) is all wrapped up in the *undergoing* (seeing the flame, feeling pain, withdrawing the hand).

Dewey believed that by examining different types of experiences, we can increase our understanding not only of experience, but of different kinds of *things*. The *things* we experience aren't just physical things, such as this chair, this computer, and that book. We also experience joy, and friendship, and disappointment. We experience a wonderful concert performance, a cocktail reception, and a first date. We experience pain, and sweetness, and a sunrise. We experience school.

DOI: 10.1057/9781137449320.0007

The last example is a telling one. What *is* a school? It's not just the physical building. Without the activities that go on there, it would just be an empty shell—like the many closed public schools here in Chicago, sitting boarded up and ghost-like throughout the city. Think about the experiences you've had of school. If you have had the opportunity to walk through an empty school building, you know that the thoughts and emotions that are brought up flavor your experience of it. A school includes students, teachers, administrators, staff, activities, learning, teaching, relationships, conflict, hall passes, football games, and chess clubs. All of these figure into school as we experience it.

Experience is of far more than just physical entities. (The word "entity" is more general than the word "thing," so I will use it to refer to everything we experience.) Love, beauty, emptiness, a favorite coffee mug, stillness, bustle, strength, a city, an argument, peace, America: these are all experienced entities. Dewey adopts James's (1909/1971) *radical* empiricism: radical because it considers *qualities* and *relations* as well as physical things. Qualities and relations are what gives reality its capacity to produce value, intentions, emotion: in short, the richness of human experience. Relations are also central to understanding systems.

> Dewey is calling us, by his use of language as well as his propositions, to relinquish a static, mechanistic picture of atomistic entities, of individuals abstracted from development, and so definitionally and definitively divided from each other such that they can only be related externally, like the parts of a machine. It is for him morally and politically significant that living calls us not to force things, or each other, out of lively relation into divisive orderings, or to treat anyone as no more than a means to a supposedly higher end or purpose (as a part has no value except as it serves to make the machine work). (Minnich, 2006, pp. 153–154)

Dewey's eclectic understanding of what counts as the "stuff" of experience has some significant implications for his overall conception of the nature of nature. At various times in his career, he refers to the attempt to develop a metaphysics or overall philosophy of the nature of nature. Dewey's metaphysics aims to be *empirical*—that is, based on experience. This chapter explores his metaphysical ideas, with particular attention to the implications these ideas have for understanding *systems*.

DOI: 10.1057/9781137449320.0007

Situations

Most importantly, we *never* experience just one entity in complete isolation from everything else. There is no such thing as an entity on its own. As the naturalist John Muir (1911/1990) put it, "When we try to pick out anything by itself, we find it hitched to everything else in the universe" (p. 110). Every entity comes with a surrounding environment, or context. (Indeed, at first encounter, we don't differentiate an entity from its context.) "Life goes on in an environment; not merely in it but because of it, through interaction with it" (Dewey, *Art as Experience*, 1934, LW 10.19). Dewey referred to the context in which we experience entities as a *situation*.

All experiences take place within one or more situations. Situations are made up of networks of relations among entities. These interrelationships are as much a part of the situations—and of our experience of them—as are the entities involved. What are these interrelationships made of? Communication (Bateson, 2011). More on that later.

An example from my own experience of schooling will help.

> When I was in third grade, at Hudson Street School in Freehold, New Jersey, my teacher, Ms. Laub, arranged a special day. She invited the students' parents to come to the class and observe a spelling bee among the class members. She was proud of the work we had done learning how to spell some difficult words, and wanted to give us an opportunity to display our prowess. I also imagine as a teacher that she hoped that if we knew the spelling bee was coming up, we'd be more diligent in preparing.
>
> I was generally an excellent speller, writer, and reader. I urged my mother to come. I distinctly remember the setup: we sat at our regular desks (arranged in rows, alphabetically) and the parents sat in a semi-circle around the back and sides of the room. There were probably 15 or 20 of them, including my mother. Ms. Laub sat on her desk (as she often did, legs crossed), stage left in the front. I remember feeling proud that my mother would see me do very well in the spelling bee.
>
> I made it through the first couple of rounds. We were in two teams: the reds and the blues. I was one of two reds left. It was my turn. Ms. Laub read out the challenge: "clift." *I knew that one*! I quickly spelled "C L I F T" and looked at her smiling, expectantly. "No, sorry Craig, the correct spelling is 'C L I F F'. Take your seat." *What?!?* I *knew* it was spelled with a T at the end: I had *heard* the T when she said the word. "But, I *know* it has a T at the end," I said, petulantly. She gestured to my desk. I sat down—a hot, uncomfortable feeling running up my neck.

DOI: 10.1057/9781137449320.0007

> The blue team ended up winning the spelling bee. There were some cupcakes and fruit punch before the parents left. My mother put her arm around my shoulders and said "Nice job!" *Not really!* I thought. I didn't feel proud at all: I felt dejected, embarrassed, and self-righteous. I still thought I was right. I tried to explain this to my mother. I think she just smiled.
>
> When I got home later, I hurried to the living room and pulled one of the two volumes of our enormous family dictionary off the shelf and quickly turned to the right page. There it was, in black and white: "cliff." My heart sank. I went upstairs to my room, closed the door, and lay down on my bed.
>
> (Nine years later, when I was a freshman in college, I had a flashback to this incident. The college library had the full *Oxford English Dictionary* [*OED*], something like 16 volumes. I looked up "cliff." There, in the long entry, I saw it: "Now chiefly dialectical: CLIFT." I was vindicated!)

This story, it must be said, is my memory of the occasion, looking back through decades. The whole situation may have been quite different (although I checked with my mother and she remembers it this way, too). But it *was*, and still *is*, a situation.

The various entities that I mentioned—Hudson Street School, my mother, Ms. Laub, her desk, the classroom, the uncomfortable feeling in my neck, the fruit punch, the family dictionary, the college library, the *OED*—can be abstracted *out* of the situation, but then they become something else: an isolated conception, a constructed object, an abstraction. In the situation, all of these entities are in a "complex web of ongoing relations" (Granger, 2006, p. 57) with all of the other entities. We experience these as a whole, as a *gestalt*.[2] These relations *constitute* the situation.

What's more, the situation I described is embedded within other situations that I could also describe, if that is what I wanted to draw your attention to: the two years and a couple of days I spent at that school, the street that both the school and our house was on, the rich history of the school building. Situations don't come prepackaged. The boundaries of a situation—what's included, and what's not—are determined by attention. What we notice is what we pay attention to. Everything else fades into the background.[3]

This last idea might cause you to say: "So the situation isn't *real*; it's just what *you* pick out of reality to focus on." Well, that depends on what you define as *real*.

Dewey develops a conception of reality that includes *us*. *We* are as much a part of reality as anything else. In our own experience, we are always there, whether we are aware of ourselves or not. "We can never

DOI: 10.1057/9781137449320.0007

speak about nature without, at the same time, speaking of ourselves" (Capra & Luisi, 2014, p. 74). What we experience is *interactions* between us and other aspects of our environment.[4] There is no experience without interaction. "Everything that exists in as far as it is known and knowable is in interaction with other things" (*Experience and Nature*, 1925, LW 1.138). Let me emphasize this: *we don't have any experience of anything unless we interact with it*. This is a central implication of Dewey's understanding of experience as *what* we experience combined with *how* we experience.[5]

Experience is the source of all our knowledge, all our memories, our values: our entire world view. Together with our genetic make-up, it is the source of *ourselves*. We *emerge* from our experiences. (Emergence is a concept we will discuss later.) Each experience has an effect on who we are. As we go through life, we experience a succession of experiences. Each one follows on another and leads to yet another. Experience is thus *continuous*.

For Dewey, *interaction* and *continuity* are essential features of experience (see Dewey's *Experience and Education*, 1938). Dewey thinks of these as the vertical and horizontal dimensions of experience. Along the horizontal dimension, imagine a timeline. It points to the right and is continuous. Along the vertical dimension is the interaction between us and everything else. What is included in that dimension varies from moment to moment.

Now let's add a bit of complexity to this image. Below the line of time put what we're *unconscious* or *unaware* of—what we're *not* paying attention to. Above the line is the situation or situations we are aware of, including the entities and relations among entities that we pay attention to. Entities and relations shift from above the line to below the line as time goes on.

Let's visualize this as a Cartesian Plane, with the "x axis" along the horizontal and the "y axis" along the vertical, with us (me, you) where the lines cross, at the *origin point* (0,0). Our awareness of the present moment (what we'll call the "foreground") is above the line (0,+y); what we're not conscious of at the present moment (the "background") is below the line (0,−y). Our past is to the left (−x,0) and our future is to the right (+x,0). Does this make sense?[6] What we've just created is a simple model of experience.

We can use this graph to help us think further about experience. Put my life along the x axis. Populate the x axis with various milestones in my life. My history began on a cold January night in 1962 while my Dad

DOI: 10.1057/9781137449320.0007

was on shore leave from the Navy. In September of that year, I emerged from my mother. Here I am, today, 52 years later. Sometime in the spring of 1971 was the spelling bee. By 1971, I was pretty different than I was in 1962—and different from how I am now. My Dad and Mom are pretty different now, too. There's a lot of history behind us.

Let's put Ms. Laub on the graph. She emerges into the foreground for the first time in the summer of 1970, when I visited Hudson Street School to meet my third grade teacher. Yes, I know, she was born long before that; but remember that this is *my* experience. Before then, she was below the line (and I have no idea what went on in her life). She remained involved in my experience to some extent until September of 1972, when we moved away. Her actual person goes under the line at that point, never to come up again. But her memory lives on in my experience, appearing occasionally above the line (like right now). We can visualize her memory as a dotted line. (Her memory, of course, isn't the same thing as her person. But it's just as real. It exists.)

The thing is, in *my* experience (and now in yours, too!), Ms. Laub herself has a history: a beginning, an ongoing series of interactions, and (at some point) an ending.

Generic traits of existences

All entities have histories. This may seem odd to say, but think about it. You *never* experience an entity as not having a history. In experience, all entities have a beginning, periods of time in which they interact with us, and an ending.

All entities, Dewey tells us, are *events*.

The spelling bee in 1971 was an event. It had a beginning, a middle, and an end. My memory of it is another event, with a history, a middle... and, eventually (not yet), an end. *I* am an event (whether it is you or me thinking about me, I'm an event regardless). *You* are an event. Hudson Street School is an event.[7]

One implication is that *time* is an aspect of all entities. Nothing occurs outside of time (as far as we know). You might think there are some entities that are by their very nature outside of time. Plato, for example, believed that the Forms—especially Truth, Beauty, and the Good—are eternal, existing outside of time. Dewey took great issue with that. Surely there was a point in history where even these "eternal" ideas were *first*

DOI: 10.1057/9781137449320.0007

conceived. Plato didn't invent the concepts. He acquired them from the culture of ancient Athens. They certainly go back hundreds or thousands of years before that. If we wanted to, we could write a history of these supposedly eternal ideas.

Dewey's word for the general "timedness" of all things is *temporality*. Temporality is one of "the generic traits manifested by existences of all kinds" (*Experience and Nature*, 1925, LW 1.308). This isn't trivial even though it is a generalization. It reminds us to think about everything as having a history. As we'll see, Dewey's attention to *time* gives his pragmatic naturalism an appreciation of the dynamic nature of reality that makes it especially applicable to systems. In particular, all *systems* are *events*, and are made up of events, and occur within the context of situations consisting of still other events. *Temporality* is an essential aspect of all systems. All systems have histories: beginnings, middles, ends. Attention to time also allows for the importance of **teleological** concepts that explain events in terms of what they lead to (*telos*) over time, such as potential, possibility, and purpose. These—as we'll see—are critical to Dewey's conception of the nature of nature.

All events occur within one or more situations, or contexts. The biggest situation—and the biggest event—is nature itself. Another way of saying this is that nature is "an affair of affairs" (LW 1.83). The affairs of experience are linked in innumerable ways with the other affairs of experience. They interact with one another.

In addition to temporality and interaction, there are other generic traits of all entities. I once identified 40 generic traits that appear somewhere in Dewey's *Collected Works* (Cunningham, 1995). This is perhaps too many to be of much use. Boisvert (1998b) whittles the list down to just four most important ones. We've already identified two: *temporality* and *interaction*. The other two identified by Boisvert are *qualitative uniqueness* and *complexity*.

Qualitative uniqueness refers to the fact that any existence is *what* it is—unlike every other event. As Dewey put it, "Events... have a phase of brute and unconditioned 'isness,' of being just what they irreducibly are.... In every event there is something obdurate, self-sufficient, wholly immediate, neither a relation nor an element in a relational whole, but terminal and exclusive" (LW 1.74). Qualities are an intrinsic and essential part of experience. "The world in which we immediately live, that in which we strive, succeed, and are defeated is preeminently a qualitative world" (Dewey, "Qualitative Thought," 1930, LW 5.243).The moment Ms.

DOI: 10.1057/9781137449320.0007

Laub told me I'd spelled that word wrong was qualitatively unique in a way I didn't ever want to repeat! It had a palpable quality that I can only describe in retrospect as *embarrassing*. That quality was *felt*, deeply. Only later did I name it (and in so doing, inevitably simplified it).

Complexity is a generic trait that is related to the others. Nothing is completely simple as it comes to us in experience, because nothing exists without interactions or without a history. And nothing is anything other than what it is. In Dewey's understanding, experience can't be *reduced* to a set of simpler building blocks, like atoms or isolated moments in time. Simples like these are abstractions: the product of *thought*. Experiences as they come to us are both spatially and temporally *complex*.

All entities interact with other entities, exhibit temporality, are qualitatively unique, and are complex. These *generic traits* define Dewey's philosophy of the nature of nature. And each of these is also a trait of every system involved in schooling.

We haven't yet fully mined Dewey's philosophy for what it can tell us about systems. There are a few other key concepts that will prove important as we go. These additional concepts come from an examination of *inquiry*.

Inquiry

Inquiry is a fundamental type of experience, deeply rooted in our existential situation as living organisms in a complex world (Godfrey-Smith, 1998). Because things constantly *change*, we are continually having to figure out ways to adapt. This is true both at the individual level and at the societal and species levels. Adaptations to change result in evolution: of species, societies, systems of all types, and individuals. Dewey was fascinated by the implications of Darwin's thinking on philosophy, writing *The Influence of Darwinism on Philosophy* in 1909, and he adopted (and adapted) Darwin's image of an organism's struggle to survive as a central metaphor of human experience.

The general method used in responding to change is inquiry.[8] Through inquiry we evolve, or learn.

The process of inquiry has a general structure. Inquiry begins with birth. This is one of the most traumatic experiences we will ever have. If it's a vaginal birth, we gradually find ourselves squeezed between our mother's pelvic bones and forced out, like toothpaste out of a tube,

DOI: 10.1057/9781137449320.0007

often into glaring light. It might take a pat on our bottom to shake us out of our amniotic stupor, but then we notice: things have changed! It is scary! We cry (thereby, unbeknownst to us, taking our first breaths). Someone cuts our umbilical cord; fortunately, we don't feel it. We cry until we are exhausted, or until something else happens—we are wiped off and wrapped in a blanket. It gets warm again. We are placed into our mother's arms. She is exhausted, but beaming. We see her face and hear her familiar voice and we calm down. She is our oasis.

Those first few moments are our first encounter with environmental change. Fortunately for us, someone else takes care of us. Unlike some other animals, we aren't born with a host of instincts that give us basic survival skills. Instead, we start out life with a body that knows what it needs (it tells us, for example, whether it is cold or hungry), is able to breathe without us thinking about it, and is able to digest our mother's milk. We are also born with a few reflexes essential for our survival: we cry when we are hungry or cold or scared; we notice and are fascinated by human faces; we suck on things that touch us near our mouths; we grasp anything that touches our palms. What's more, by the time we are born, we have already learned a few things inside our mothers' wombs. We recognize her voice; we pay attention to her; we are soothed by her calmness and upset with her upset. We have become habituated to her movements, and are able to move parts of ourselves as well, although we haven't quite figured out yet how to control those movements. But the most important thing we have when we are born is "plasticity"—"the capacity to retain and carry over from prior experience factors which modify subsequent activities. This signifies the capacity to acquire habits, or develop definite dispositions" (Dewey, *Democracy and Education*, 1916, MW 9.51). Plasticity makes it possible for us to *grow*.

From these modest beginnings—and with the help of our mothers and other people we encounter—we gradually construct our world. How? By responding to change, through inquiry, and being reshaped by it.

When we are born, we aren't simply passive. Healthy infants are active, vital, moving, and responsive. The few reflexes and the habits we have already acquired operate constantly: they are "projective, dynamic in quality, ready for overt manifestation; and... operative in some subdued subordinate form even when not obviously dominating activity" (Dewey, *Human Nature and Conduct*, 1922, MW 14.32). Throughout our lives, during moments of stability and routine, it is our habits that keep us

DOI: 10.1057/9781137449320.0007

going. We daydream or let our minds wander, aimlessly—like life in the womb.

But when something changes in our environment, like birth—or even a simple thing like we've dropped our favorite toy—we notice! We become alert and pay attention. When we're infants, our inquiry skills are limited. We are upset! We cry! Dad comes over and asks "What's the matter, snugglebuns?" He sees the toy, lying right next to us. He picks it up. "It's right here!" He shows it to us, puts it back in our hand, and smiles. We calm down. "Are you okay now, snugglebuns?"

As we get older, we develop more nuanced ways to handle change. Fast forward to third grade. Notice how much we have learned. We talk and read and write. We walk to school, play with our friends, sit at our desks and listen, fill out worksheets, raise our hands, ask for a pass if we need to go to the bathroom, remember our homework (some of the time), and learn how spell "cliff." Some of us, anyway.

Instead of just crying when we find ourselves upset, we have learned a more sophisticated approach. We ask, *is the change important? Does it affect me?* If it's nothing to worry about, our minds settle back into idleness. If it's important, we inquire. We survey what's going on. We examine the various entities in our immediate environment, trying to figure out what's happened. We *situate* ourselves; that is, we construct or assemble a situation.

As I spelled out "C L I F T," I wasn't thinking, really. I *knew* how to spell that word. I was just going through the motions, on cruise control. My mind was focused on the presence of my mother. I even stole a sly glance at her as if to say *I've got this!* But then, when Ms. Laub said, "Sorry, Craig..." everything changed! Suddenly I wasn't happy. I tried to argue with Ms. Laub. I pouted. I tried to get my mother to take my side over a cup of fruit punch.

The rest of the day, as school went on around me, I continued my inquiry. *How can I restore my dignity?* (I probably wasn't thinking those exact words.) I searched my mind for a solution, for something that would ease my upset. I knew that if I could just prove that my spelling was correct, everything would be okay! Finally, my thoughts began to focus on the family dictionary. I *knew* I would find my preferred spelling in there! My pace walking home was quicker than usual. I didn't stop in the corner store for a piece of candy. When I walked in the house, I didn't say "hi" to my mom. I was on a mission.

DOI: 10.1057/9781137449320.0007

It is important to notice that when Ms. Laub said "Sorry...," it wasn't just my knowledge of how to spell "cliff" that was at issue. From my perspective, my *entire life* was suddenly on the line. At that moment, I *became* a person on a mission of inquiry. Even though I had to participate in the rest of the school day, my mind wasn't really there. The situation I was in was elsewhere: I was minding *that* situation.

Again, you may be thinking: "No, the situation you were in was in class, at school. Your *internal* state of mind doesn't change that fact." Yes, my *body* might have been in class: everyone would agree on that. But from my perspective, so what? Of course, if something happened in class that required my attention—Ms. Laub calling on me for an answer to 8 × 7—I might have temporarily parachuted back in, said my answer, and then flew back out again. If I got it *wrong*—and I very well might have, since that particular math fact eluded me until years later—I would be forced to stay in class a bit longer and attend to *that* situation. I might have found myself—like many students do—in *two* situations at once, both of them affecting my self-esteem. (Keep this in mind as we discuss the complexity of schooling: students have a variety of stuff going on in their lives; they are not *just* students in a given classroom.)

Dewey referred to the situation that emerges immediately upon noticing a change in our environments or in ourselves as an *indeterminate situation*. It's *indeterminate* because at first we have no idea what is going on.[9] What makes it "indeterminate"? We don't *know*; that's what we try to find out—through inquiry.

Inquiry is:

> ...the controlled or directed transformation of an indeterminate situation into one that is so determinate in its constituent distinctions and relations as to convert the elements of the original situation into a unified whole. (*Logic: The Theory of Inquiry*, 1938, LW 12.108)

This is an important quotation. Let's look at it closely.

We examine the "distinctions and relations" that "constitute" the situation. These are what might help us to resolve the indeterminacy. This usually involves breaking the situation up—analyzing it—into distinct parts, separate entities. As I've said, these become separate and distinct only as a *result* of inquiry. *We make* distinctions as we construct the situation. This is a matter of what Dewey called "selective emphasis" (LW 1.34). We don't look at everything. What we choose to look at is driven

DOI: 10.1057/9781137449320.0007

by a particular inquiry; but it is also a matter of what we value and desire (Granger, 2006). This is important to remember: what we pay attention to isn't the whole of reality. This is why we refer to everything we aren't currently conscious of as "background." We make no distinctions in the background. To speak of things that are in the background as separate entities is to bring them to the foreground. But the background is still there.

To separate parts out for examination, we either apply a distinction that we have acquired from previous experience or we create a new one. Once we have extracted a particular part of the situation as a distinct entity, we examine its *relations* with everything else in the situation. Does it relate to the indeterminacy? If not, it recedes back into background. If it does seem related, it becomes part of the foreground. As we assemble the situation in the foreground, we *simplify*. We only pay attention to what seems relevant—what seems related to what matters. As Gregory Bateson (2000/1972) put it, we pay attention to the "difference that makes a difference" (p. 315).

Notice something I said a few paragraphs ago: inquiry begins when we notice a change *in our environments or in ourselves*. When we operate out of habit, the distinction between ourselves and our environment doesn't exist. Even *that* distinction has to be *made* through inquiry. Bateson gives an excellent example of why making a distinction between ourselves and our environment isn't always simple or obvious. Imagine a blind man, using a stick to walk. He holds the stick in front of him as he walks, using it to feel obstacles or unevenness in his path to prevent crashing into them or tripping. Is the stick part of the environment or part of the man? This is what I mean by making distinctions. These are generally *up to us*—not given to us by an external world (Bateson, 2000/1972; Hutchins, 2010).

This brings me back to what I said about the possibility of applying a distinction that we have previously acquired. We don't encounter every indeterminate situation in our lives in the same way. As we experience more and more, we evolve; we grow; we *learn*. One of the things we *learn* is distinctions and relations that work in various circumstances. These are stabilities in an otherwise unstable world, and they are "means of control, of enlarged use of and enjoyment of ordinary things" (LW 1.17). Without some such stabilities in the world, learning would not be possible.

As I mentioned above, every experience follows another and precedes yet another, continuously. These continuities affect who we

DOI: 10.1057/9781137449320.0007

are. Something that we experience again and again becomes familiar to us. We develop routine ways of responding to it. These routines, over time, develop into habits. When we encounter that something again, we already *know* how to deal with it. Indeed, our habitual capacity to handle it might be such that it never even arises into our awareness: it remains in the background.

Habits

Habits continuously operate in the background. They don't go away just because we aren't thinking about them. By handling things for us, habits allow us to go through life without paying attention to *everything* (which would get old pretty fast).

Some habits develop in our bodies. For example, I go up the same set of stairs every time I come home to my apartment. The stairs twist around 180 degrees. Each stair is a slightly different shape. Some of them are pointed at one end, so there's barely any stair there. If you try to step on a part of a stair that isn't there, you trip. When I first moved in, I tripped multiple times. I had been habituated to stairs that all have the same shape. These stairs confused my stair-climbing habits. But now, I know how to climb those stairs, without thinking. To be more precise, I should say that my body knows, or my habits know.

Some habits develop in our minds. I *knew* how to spell *clift*. I had spelled it many times. When Ms. Laub said the word, I *heard* the T at the end. When I said it to myself over and over later that day, there was a T there! This illustrates the way we often apply the word "habit" to a *bad* habit. My habit of spelling *cliff* with a T was a bad habit, because it put me in a situation I did not want to be in. Later, after I failed to find my preferred spelling in the family dictionary, I resigned myself to learning how to spell it as C L I F F. Even in third grade, I had heard that the only way to cure a bad habit is to develop a new one. So I worked on developing a new habit. I said the word correctly to myself. I wrote it out a few times. For the next decade, every time I encountered the word I had to consciously replace that T with an F. But eventually, I learned: spelling *cliff* correctly became a habit.

Both of these examples show how habits work. Our initial encounter with a situation doesn't go so well. We don't want to repeatedly stumble. From that time forward, we pay closer attention when similar challenges arise. If we find a different way to respond that works, we repeat that different way until it becomes automatic. Gradually, the challenge fades into the background.

DOI: 10.1057/9781137449320.0007

We grow by developing habits. This is how we learn. The process is self-correcting: habits that don't work for us get changed. If two habits come into conflict, that becomes an indeterminate situation, and we inquire to synthesize a new habit. The process is iterative: a new habit is formed by doing something over and over. The process is additive: as we move through our lives, we acquire more and more habits. The process is *cybernetic*; it's a learning system, and it produces a system of habits.[10]

The "interpenetration of habits" (MW 14.30) that we develop—which Dewey referred to as our *character*—makes up the automatic or unconscious ways we respond to ongoing experience. This interpenetration provides an "immediate, seemingly instinctive, feeling of the direction and end of various lines of behavior" (MW 14.26), enabling a mature person to respond to ongoing events in consistent yet adaptable ways. "Interpenetration" is an interesting and seldom-seen word. It implies that the system of habits we develop is deeply interconnected within itself.

So when I said that the distinction between ourselves and our environment is something we have to *make*, realize that the distinction itself may become a habit. We may habitually make the distinction in the same way. Then, the only time we have to think about it is when the distinction doesn't work.

In that case, we inquire. We make distinctions and examine relations. Like an artist working with a piece of clay, we *work* the situation. If we are able to transform it into a situation that is determinate, we're done. We forget about it and move on. But if during our inquiry, we discover something about the situation that isn't right—something out of place, a missing part, a distinction we are having trouble making, a relation we don't understand, an expected outcome that isn't happening—we may define a *problem*. We then say that the situation is "problematic."

What is the problem? We define it as we work on the situation. As I thought about my embarrassment at the spelling bee, I defined a problem: I had to prove to Ms. Laub that I was *right*. I worked on how to solve that problem. My chosen solution: looking in the dictionary. Once I'd seen that *she* was right, I lay on my bed, dejected. Once I was done feeling sorry for myself, I developed a new way of looking at the situation. I redefined the problem: I had to learn how to spell *cliff* correctly.

Keep this in mind: we don't encounter problems fully formed. Rather, we encounter moments when our path forward is blocked. We then

DOI: 10.1057/9781137449320.0007

construct indeterminate situations. During this process, any problems involved have to be defined. That is the first step toward solving them.[11]

Knowing

Most people don't think of knowledge as a type of habit, but it is. Above, I described how my *knowledge* that *cliff* was spelled with a T at the end was habitual. It was also wrong. It was a habit that had to be changed. The habit that replaced it—spelling *cliff* in the correct way—was correct knowledge.

Knowledge is made up of distinctions and relations acquired from our experience that we can use in multiple situations. Dewey wanted to challenge the common notion of knowledge as mental "stuff," and encouraged speaking of *knowing* as an active, situated, practical affair. Gert Biesta (2007) writes:

> Dewey's transactional understanding of experience provides a framework in which knowing is no longer about an immaterial mind looking at the material world and registering what goes on in it—a view to which Dewey referred as the spectator theory of knowledge. For him, knowing is not about a world "out there," but concerns the relation between our actions and their consequences—which is the central idea of Dewey's transactional theory of knowing. (p. 13)

Like the child's knowledge of what a flame will do to her finger or my knowledge of how to spell *cliff*, all knowledge is a result of action. *All knowledge is about relations* (whether actual relations or potential relations). Distinctions are a type of relation. "To know something is to be aware of what might happen to it, what behavior to expect, what results will follow, what expectations to assume, under specified conditions" (Boisvert, 1998a, p. 24). Acts of knowing that prove useful to us in multiple situations become habitual. In practical terms, knowledge consists of associations in our minds—gathered from prior experience—that connect an event with some possible future. Knowing these possible relationships is what helps us predict what might happen. The capacity to become aware of potential consequences, our "potential awareness" as it were, is therefore the crux of pure and applied knowledge. Without an awareness of potential consequences, we would be powerless to control the course of events, and powerless to understand experience. All experience would be immediate (not mediated), and we would have no ability, or means, to direct or control nature.

Knowing is what gives events their meaning.

DOI: 10.1057/9781137449320.0007

Meaning

When an event has meaning, it triggers associations in our minds with possibilities: potential consequences. We can therefore speak of "events-with-meaning." After the child burned her finger, she sees the flame differently: it is in Dewey's words "funded" with meaning.

> When an event has meaning, its potential consequences become its integral and funded feature. When the potential consequences are important and repeated, they form the very nature and essence of a thing, its defining, identifying, and distinguishing form.... To perceive is to acknowledge unattained possibilities; it is to refer the present to consequences...and thereby to behave in deference to the connections of events. (*Experience and Nature*, 1925, LW 1.143)

Meanings connect events to possibilities. "When we name an event, calling it fire, we speak proleptically; we do not name an immediate event; that is impossible. We employ a term of discourse; we invoke a meaning, namely, the potential consequence of the existence" (LW 1.150). "Fire" *means* potential pain, burning, melting, or warmth. It means other things to other people in other situations. Its possible meanings are only limited to the number of different ways someone discovers it can lead to something.

In assigning meanings to events, we confer "upon things traits and potentialities which did not previously belong to them"; this assignment "marks a change by which physical events exhibiting properties of mechanical energy...realize characters, meanings and relations of meanings hitherto not possessed by them" (LW 1.285). "Meaning emerges as [an] organism organizes, controls, and directs the various existential relations (ideational and materials) that exist within the unanalyzed totality of experience" (Granger, 2006, p. 28). Meanings move events beyond mere indeterminateness; they suggest tendencies, or possible directions. Meanings are imputed potentialities, and are created in the application of intelligence to experience.

Meanings bring the future into the present. What I mean by this will become clearer as we go.

Intelligence

Just as Dewey reconstructs knowledge as practical, active, and situated, he also transforms the traditional meaning of **intelligence**. Minds are

DOI: 10.1057/9781137449320.0007

situated as much as any other existent. Intelligence therefore requires taking careful account of situations, which include bodies, emotions and complex contexts. Intelligence creates meaning and relations of meaning and applies these relations in new situations.

Dewey's understanding of intelligence is very different from the way that behaviorist psychologists have defined it, as a simple, measurable quality:

> A man is intelligent not in virtue of having reason which grasps first and indemonstrable truths about fixed principles, in order to reason deductively from them to the particulars which they govern, but in virtue of his capacity to estimate the possibilities of a situation and to act in accordance with his estimate. In the large sense of the term, intelligence is as practical as reason is theoretical. (Dewey, *Quest for Certainty*, 1929, LW 4.170)

Intelligence is a result of a varied set of virtues or habits: character. Jackson (2002) describes this in human terms:

> What does a masterful exercise of intelligence...actually take? To begin, it takes a host of personal dispositions, habits, and attitudes—among them patience, persistence, open-mindedness, careful observation, unflagging attention to detail, reflection, experimentation, imagination, an abiding faith in one's own capacity to pursue the truth, an enduring delight in that pursuit, and even—all cautious proprieties aside—an undying love of it. (p. 81)

These are the sorts of qualities that should be developed through schooling.

The "masterful exercise of intelligence" also leaves room for tremendous range of variation and diversity in any population. As I said above, change is the only guaranteed constant. Intelligence that expects and incorporates the various changes going on in any complex environment is going to be more responsive and more capable than intelligence that operates as if everything stays more or less the same, which is fundamentally a *simplification* of reality based on *abstraction*. Bowers (2012) refers to this more capable type of intelligence as *ecological* intelligence. As we'll see, this is particularly valuable in understanding complex systems.

Howard Gardner's (1999) theory of multiple intelligences suggests that what has traditionally been viewed as intelligence is too limiting, that in addition to logical-mathematical and linguistic intelligence, there are also musical, bodily-kinesthetic, spatial, interpersonal, intrapersonal, and naturalist (ecological) intelligences. This offers a more pluralistic

DOI: 10.1057/9781137449320.0007

understanding of intelligence that captures what many non-Western cultures believe (Kezar, 2005). It is also much more compatible with Dewey's view, and it also leaves room for emotions to play a role.

> Thinking is always rooted in the total process of psychic activity. There is no thinking without emotion. We get angry, for example, when we can't solve a problem, and our anger influences our thinking. Thought is embedded in a context of feeling and affect; thought influences, and is in turn influenced by, that context. (Dörner, 1997, p. 8)

The emotional and motivational aspects of intelligence make sense if we remember that all thinking is situated, arising in a context of participation in the affairs of the world—a participation that involves "emotions, intentions, intuitions, desires, needs, and habits" which "make up the non-cognitive background, from which all conscious thinking and acting emerge" (Lehmann-Rommel, 2000, pp. 191–192). Like all other existences, emotion is embedded in situations. As always, the interrelationships that emotions have with other entities in the environment—that is, their communications—are crucial to what those emotions mean.

In general, our culture tends to over-value cognition, relative to the other important aspects of intelligence. My embarrassment at misspelling *cliff* was as much part of the situation as the cognitive activity that led to checking the dictionary, or deciding to habituate the correct spelling. Emotion implicates the body and thus tends to draw attention to *embodied intelligence*, which, it must be said, is really the only kind.

Imagination

The importance of intelligence in inquiry should not lead us to ignore the similarly central role of imagination. Imagination makes it possible to create new ways of being in the world; without it, we are stuck in doing what we already do.

Imagination allows inquiry to be "active, associative/metaphorical, open-ended, unpredictable, and improvisational, and allows for the emergence of the new" (Marshall, 2014, p. 125). It allows for "**poiesis**," a kind of creative emergence that occurs seemingly suddenly when a system transforms into something quite different from what it was. This occurs at the moment of inquiry when a person has an "Aha!" moment and sees how an indeterminate or problematic situation can be transformed. (It can also emerge from group inquiries; see below.)

DOI: 10.1057/9781137449320.0007

The key idea in Dewey's conception of imagination is the relationship between the *actual* situation and its possibilities. Once the "constituent distinctions and relations" of a situation are mapped, we use imagination to project these constituent factors forward, to see where they might lead given a variety of different scenarios, including those involving us taking various actions. We play out the consequences of our actions in imagination *before* we enact them for real. A cultivated imagination is capable of seeing "the space of the possible" in any situation (Davis & Phelps, 2004, p. 4).

As I sat in class after the fateful spelling bee, scheming in my head, my imagination was going wild. I was imagining all the different ways that I could convince Ms. Laub that my spelling of *cliff* was correct. I could ask my mother to write a note. I could get a geology professor from the local college to call her. I could get the President of the US to decree that the alternative spelling should always be accepted. I could bribe Ms. Laub.

We evaluate the possibilities by imagining the effect of different consequences in terms of our own desires or values as they emerge in inquiry. Dewey referred to these as our "ends-in-view." Imagination recognizes the temporal direction of an event—where it has been, where it is, where it is going—and produces a conscious appraisal of the event's possibilities in relation to our ends-in-view.

Imagination enters experience as the identification of "the possibilities that are interwoven within the texture of the actual" (LW 10.348). It is the primary tool for realizing what is not present. As Dewey wrote in *A Common Faith* (1934), "The only meaning that can be assigned the term 'imagination' is that things unrealized in fact come home to us and have power to stir us" (LW 9.30). Elements of the possible future enter present experience through imagination, and enable us to transform the future into what we desire.

As Garrison (1995) puts it, "The existential task is to create a cosmos from chaos by guiding indeterminate events in new directions that promote prosperity" (p. 356). Generally, the ideal is to resolve the indeterminacy of the situation in a way that secures desired goods: things we want, or value.

Values

Dewey writes:

> Our constant and inescapable concern is with prosperity and adversity, success and failure, achievement and frustration, good and bad. Since we are

DOI: 10.1057/9781137449320.0007

> creatures with lives to live, and find ourselves within an uncertain environment, we are constructed to note and judge in terms of bearing upon weal and woe—upon value. [This] presents something *to be accomplished*, to be brought about by the *actions* in which choice is manifested and made genuine. (*Experience and Nature*, 1925, LW 1.33)

Experience presents us with immediate desires. But how do we decide which goods are actually valuable? This is a matter of "evaluative thinking," which Dewey discussed in *Theory of Valuation* (1939).

As mentioned above, Dewey believed that qualities are intrinsic to experience: they are immediately felt. We encounter qualities in every situation. Some of those qualities are immediately attractive to us and some are repulsive. These immediate responses are indicative of native preferences or previously acquired habits. But the mere "fact that something is desired only raises the *question* of its desirability; it does not settle it" (LW 4.208). To settle the question requires that we take the time to engage in inquiry about the desirability of an end in light of the means necessary to obtain it and the consequences which ensue from obtaining it. A truly desirable end will "make a greater contribution to enriching the quality of meaning of related situations and attendant goods" (Granger, 2006, p. 78). Thus, for Dewey, there is no intrinsic distinction between fact and value. We may make such a distinction if it serves the purposes of an inquiry, but it isn't *there* already in the nature of nature (Putnam, 2002).

Emphasizing interrelationships and qualities, as Dewey does, collapses the strong distinction between scientific objectivity and the realm of spiritual values. Dewey tried to draw attention to the role of imagination and ideals in religious experience in his *A Common Faith* (1934), a book that received a very critical reception, especially among theologians. In that book, Dewey defined God as the "uniting of the ideal and the real" (Rockefeller, 1991, p. 536), putting the emphasis on *uniting* as an active and continuous process. This conception captured Dewey's own lifelong quest to see himself as connected to reality as a whole. His understanding of immediate experience as holistic, his conception of inquiry as a process of restoring unity to indeterminate situations, and the way in which we can use our sense of possibilities as tools for securing desired goods, can be seen as aspects of this religious or spiritual quest.

DOI: 10.1057/9781137449320.0007

Social inquiry

My discussion so far of inquiry, habits, intelligence, and values has been fundamentally flawed.

How?

It ignores the *social* aspects. Inquiry is often a collective enterprise. Habits aren't just individual: they are social (as traditions or customs). Intelligence can be collective as well as individual. Communities are characterized by values that are held in common. Language—which plays a central role in experience—is social. "Shared experience is the greatest of human goods" (LW 1.157).

Consider, for example, the way that science advances. An indeterminate situation arises. No one knows how to explain it. Someone defines the problem, which presents itself to the community of scientists. They all know it's a problem that needs to be solved, and they each work on it, in their own ways. Bit by bit, pieces of a solution are proposed. Findings are published and retested by others. Eventually, someone finds a way to put the pieces together in a new way of understanding the situation.

A similar dynamic can occur in a classroom organized around inquiry. Perhaps the teacher proposes a problem: "How can Hudson Street School reduce its carbon footprint?" The class brainstorms a list of possible solutions. There are ten different possibilities given. Which ones are the most effective?

Teams are formed to inquire into each possibility. The teacher provides a rubric, providing criteria for the investigations. The teams refer to the rubric as they work. It says that each team must identify at least three affordances and three constraints for each possible action. There are other criteria, but let's focus on this.

The teacher wants "affordances" and "constraints." What are those? They are *words*. But what do they *mean?* Words are a particular kind of tool for Dewey. They are stand-ins for entities and meanings. We imbue them with significance by understanding what they signify—sometimes habitually.

An **affordance** is what a given action, tool, or method can *do*. A **constraint** is what that action, tool, or method might *limit* us from doing. One of the proposed actions is for Hudson Street School to permanently shut off its furnace. One affordance of this is that it would cut carbon

DOI: 10.1057/9781137449320.0007

emissions dramatically. But a constraint is that on cold days the teachers and students would be wearing their coats and hats and gloves, unable to think very well about affordances and constraints or anything else.

How are these words *helpful*? By putting them on the rubric, the teacher has directed every student's attention to the possibilities and limitations of alternative actions, giving their inquiry some guidelines. We can say that these guidelines are a type of *scaffold*.

Words allow us to quickly convey a distinction or a relation that has shown itself to work in varied situations. When we learn a word, we gain access to the power of prediction and control that it conveys. Words themselves have both affordances and constraints. Language is an enormous shared reservoir of distinctions and relations that has been built up over time. It is, as Dewey says, "the tool of tools" (LW 1.146). But we also unconsciously adopt understandings that are embedded in words. For example, depending on the way a teacher uses a word like "tradition," it may be seen as an unreflective and outmoded choice or as deep wisdom. Similarly, the word "technology" may be used to refer to inevitable progress, or as a tool that can be used for good or evil depending on a person's goals. Teachers don't always consider the implications of how they use such words (Bowers, 2012). This is one reason that a good education includes learning a second language.

Social inquiry at its best is democratic, giving each unique person involved a voice that enriches the larger conversation with diverse perspectives, allowing "a broad forum for negotiating between these orientations without positing any single one as universal or final. The most important issue for Dewey is how we develop and maintain such a forum for inquiry" in the larger society, in schools, and in classrooms (Granger, 2006, p. 75). Granger continues, "Time and experience have shown that goods such as shared activity and open and free communication, goods that Dewey regularly associates with democratic life, are very likely to strengthen and diversify our relations with our everyday environments" (pp. 88–89). Or as Dewey puts it, "Variety is the spice of life, and the richness and the attractiveness of social institutions depend upon cultural diversity.... In so far as people are all alike, there is no give and take among them. And it is better to give and take" ("The Principle of Nationality," 1917, MW 10.288). Diversity strengthens any system, and leaving open the question of what is best allows for democratic discourse, which allows for multiple perspectives and enables flexible social inquiry which has the best chance of solving the complex problems our society faces.

DOI: 10.1057/9781137449320.0007

An example

Let me offer an example that demonstrates a pragmatic approach to situated social inquiry in schools.

At Frederick Douglass High School, located in a major Midwest city, students assemble portfolios that reflect the progress of their academic work throughout the year.[12] By looking at the portfolios, teachers and community members (including parents) assess each student's growth. They make *judgments* about that growth. (This is a type of evaluative thinking.) These judgments are written up in detailed reports that accompany student report cards. All assessment reports are reviewed by a member of the school's leadership team—which includes department chairs and administrators—who sometimes make suggestions about rewriting the reports to make them more useful to the students. Once the reports are rewritten, the reports are also entered into the students' files, and are used by guidance counselors and others to write college and job recommendations for the students toward the end of their senior year.

How are the judgments made?

Typically, a three-member assessment panel that includes two teachers and one community member or parent assesses the portfolio, following a presentation of the portfolio by the student.

Their assessment is not made solely based on what is contained in the portfolio. Rather, the assessment panel thinks about what is in the portfolio in terms of a detailed rubric of assessment *criteria*. These criteria have been determined systematically, taking account of the goals, processes, and values of the school community. They have been made available to the students from the first day of their freshman orientation, and are referred to often as they assemble their portfolios (MacLellan, 1999; Greenberg, 2004).

In making decisions about what to include in the portfolios, students have considered how each item might fit within the overall picture presented by the portfolio, reflecting particular aspects of academic growth. The students are encouraged to consider the criteria as they select evidence to be included. Their portfolio advisor (who is also their homeroom teacher, who stays with them throughout their four years at the school) assists the students with these decisions, and devotes time to helping students understand the expectations and how those expectations change during the four years. The students look at both the

DOI: 10.1057/9781137449320.0007

individual items in the portfolio and at the overall balance of the picture they are presenting. The assessment panel looks at the same.

Note that the *criteria* applied in the school's portfolio assessment are *not* the same as the state curriculum standards that are measured through the standardized tests that every student must pass in order to graduate. The difference between standards and criteria was well explained by Elliot Eisner (1995):

> Standards fix expectations; **criteria** are guidelines that enable one to search more efficiently for the *qualities* that might matter in any individual work.... To say that by the end of a course students will be able to write a convincing essay on the competing interests of environmentalists and industrialists that marshals good arguments supported by relevant facts is to identify criteria that can be used to appraise the essay; it is not to provide a standard for measuring it.
>
> ...The *qualities* that define *inventive* work of any kind are *qualities* that by definition have both *unique* and useful features. The particular form those features take and what it is that makes them useful are not necessarily predictable, but *sensitive* critics—and *sensitive* teachers—are able to discover such properties in the work. Teachers who know the students they teach recognize the *unique qualities* in students' comments, in their paintings, in the essays they write, in the ways in which they relate to their peers. (p. 758; my emphasis)

Notice the words "qualities," "unique," "inventive" and "sensitive." These are central aspects of criteria, but seldom found in "standards." It is important to consider why.

I would say that these words are not included in standards statements because they are considered *personal, subjective, not measurable.* But do qualities, uniqueness, inventiveness, and sensitivity *matter* in schools? The answer is obvious. They do.

But back to the portfolio assessment.

If the assessment panel concludes that a particular student has shown enormous growth in her capacity to write clearly, but has shown less growth in her capacity to express her feelings in her creative writing, the panel will support this judgment with references to specific pieces of evidence from the portfolio.

The leadership team will make its own judgment about the panel's assessment, and may suggest changes in the wording or ask for a bit more evidence for a particular assertion. Sometimes, there is some back-and-forth between the panel and the leadership team, resulting in

DOI: 10.1057/9781137449320.0007

a more complete and balanced assessment. Due to these revisions, when the student or her parents read the assessment, they often find themselves in substantial agreement with the overall assessment, and may be motivated to try to improve in the areas suggested. This is especially important in the first three years of high school, when students have an opportunity to improve their work in relation to the criteria.

So what does this example do for us?

It illustrates a few key ideas that are relevant to understanding schooling:

- The process is naturalistic: evidence is included and valued, but it is not expected to speak for itself. Like all events, the evidence is treated as embedded in one or more situations.
- Any assertion about the quality of student work is judged or evaluated in terms of the situation in which the work was made and then assessed. There is no attempt to ignore the context.
- Standardization of the assessment is never the primary goal. Assessing each student fairly and intentionally is the goal.
- Judgments are based not just upon the evidence but on the relation between the evidence and the criteria. We can say the judgments are criteria-referenced, rather than norm-referenced (Reigeluth, 2004).
- The criteria are formed not arbitrarily, but through a community-wide, democratic process.
- The overall assessment is held to be important enough that multiple people are involved in an iterative back-and-forth.
- The process of assessment is pragmatic: it recognizes there may be multiple perspectives with different judgments.
- The communication of the overall assessment includes attention to the inclusion of specific references to the evidence so that the student and her parents can understand and accept the assessment.
- The assessment acknowledges the unique nature and potential of each student, and allows for variation in the evidence used to decide whether a student has met the criteria. Equality of treatment is not important; relevance of the comments to the particular student's growth is important. This acknowledges that humans are not interchangeable parts.
- This process recognizes and accepts the complexity and situatedness of judgments about growth.

DOI: 10.1057/9781137449320.0007

- The process embraces situativity, quality, intentionality, relations, democracy, iteration, multiple perspectives, uniqueness, diversity, interaction, and complexity.
- And the process is systematic.

Notes

1 Boisvert's *John Dewey: Rethinking our Time* (1998a) is an excellent introduction to Dewey's overall philosophical work, and I highly recommend it to anyone who wants to go beyond the limits of the present book.

2 **Gestalt** is a German word that describes a pattern of interrelationships that constitute a perception of a whole. It was coined by Christian von Ehrenfels who also first said what could be the motto of systems theory: "the whole is more than the sum of its parts."

3 An excellent example is given in Bateson (2011). Look at your hand. Do you see five fingers? Or do you see the four spaces between them? In some ways, those four spaces are far more important: they allow movement and dexterity.

4 Because Dewey recognized the complexity of interactions, he came to prefer the term "**transactions**," which emphasizes multiple interactions embedded within a larger context.

5 The shaping of our experience by our personal involvement has been understood by philosophers at least since Rene Descartes. Most significantly, physicist Werner Heisenberg established what he called the Principle of Indeterminacy (or "Uncertainty Principle") in 1927. It basically says that our presence affects whatever it is we are looking at, and thereby introduces uncertainty into every measurement. The implications of this for a theory of knowing are profound.

6 If this doesn't make sense, you should pause and draw a diagram of what I'm talking about. If you don't remember what a Cartesian Plane is or this is all completely confusing, you may need to bone up on your basic algebra and geometry. I'm serious. Galileo said, "The book of nature is written in mathematics." You can't fully comprehend nature—or systems in schooling—without it. (See http://thonyc.wordpress.com/2010/07/13/the-book-of-nature-is-written-in-the-language-of-mathematics/.)

7 Hudson Street School was built in 1875. It was a venerable building, judging from the photo on the Internet: http://freeholdnj.homestead.com/files/fhs.JPG.

8 It could be said that the *reason* we inquire is *because* experience involves constant change, or complexity. See Godfrey-Smith (1998).

DOI: 10.1057/9781137449320.0007

9 Dewey also allowed that a situation could lead to inquiry if it was unsettled, doubtful, hazardous, precarious, uncertain, out of balance, or in disequilibrium. Indeterminacy is simply the archetypal quality that leads to inquiry.

10 **Cybernetics** is the science of how systems control themselves using communication. Information about conditions in one part of the system is communicated (via feedback) to another part and is used to adjust the rate or functions of various processes. Norbert Wiener (1950), the founder of cybernetics, studied with John Dewey at one time and Steg (1996) suggests that Dewey's ideas had an important influence on Wiener's ideas.

11 Later, when we talk about improving schools, we will see that school leaders can't just go from problem to problem, solving them individually. Real school improvement requires looking at systems holistically: as situations.

12 The name of the school has been changed.

DOI: 10.1057/9781137449320.0007

3
Systems

Abstract: *Some definitions related to understanding systems are given, and different types of systems are described. Some generic traits of systems are discussed, including processes, interactions, integration, and emergence. A special type of system known as a "complex adaptive system," which is the kind found in social systems such as schools, is explored. The special attributes of complex systems, including levels and time, are described, as well as messes and wicked problems.*

Cunningham, Craig A. *Systems Theory for Pragmatic Schooling: Toward Principles of Democratic Education.* New York: Palgrave Macmillan, 2014.
DOI: 10.1057/9781137449320.0008.

Before we return to schooling, we need to develop a general understanding of systems. As we do this, it is important to remember what Dewey taught us about the nature of nature. I think you'll agree that his understanding and that of systems theory are remarkably compatible.

Let's begin with defining some basic terms.

Definitions

A **system** is an arrangement of entities and their *interrelationships* such that there are some regularities or interactions in the ways that the entities behave and such that a *boundary* can be defined between what is considered inside the system and what is considered outside the system (i.e. in its environment). As illustrated with the example from Bateson of the blind man and the stick, defining such boundaries is not simply a matter of seeing what is there, but in making distinctions that work for our purposes.

Systems are structured by internal interrelationships and also by relations—or communications—with external systems. Thinking about systems "means a shift of perception from material objects and structures to the nonmaterial processes and patterns of organization" (Capra & Luisi, 2014, p. 79). Systems exhibit behaviors: they respond to inputs by producing outputs, and like everything else in nature, they change over time, or evolve.

Systems theory is a set of concepts and tools that have applicability across a variety of domains of inquiry, ranging from engineering to ecology to human development. Developed originally by Alexander Bogdanov and Ludwig von Bertalanffy and extended by Béla H. Bánáthy and others, systems theory offers a general understanding of the philosophy, theory, methodology, and application of systems. Systems theory aims for the broadest possible set of principles and approaches; it seeks to understand systems in general and systems of all types.

Essential features of systems theory include attention to wholes as well as parts. It is difficult—if not impossible—to understand a whole system by looking only at its parts. In this way, systems are like situations. Systems theory also focuses on relations and interactions among systems and subsystems, a recognition that systems don't typically operate in isolation from their environment, the appreciation of complex types of interaction involving time, and an appreciation of context. Again, these

DOI: 10.1057/9781137449320.0008

features remind us of Dewey's understanding of events. Systems theory emphasizes the development and use of models to simplify complexity (without overly reducing it).

We can distinguish several different ways of thinking about systems: there is "systemic thinking," "systematic thinking," and "systems thinking." **Systemic thinking** examines qualities, behavior, or properties that are found throughout a system, rather than in a particular, localized place or part. Systemic thinking therefore looks at patterns across all the components of a system. **Systematic thinking** refers to thinking that is not haphazard or *ad hoc*, but proceeds in a careful, step-by-step manner. Both are different from "**systems thinking**," which is the *application* of systems theory to a particular phenomenon or interrelated set of phenomena, often to solve particular problems or to transform particular systems toward optimization.

Another way to put this is that *systems theory* is *systemic thinking* about how *systems thinking* can be used *systematically* to improve *systems*. Or as Peter Senge (1990/2006) put it:

> Systems thinking is a discipline for seeing wholes. It is a framework for seeing interrelationships rather than things, for seeing patterns of change rather than static "snapshots." And systems thinking is a sensibility—for the subtle interconnectedness that gives living systems their unique character. (pp. 68–69)

Systems analysis is the application of systems theory to the analysis of specific systems. This involves enumerating the elements of the system, identifying the inputs and the outputs, mapping the interrelationships of the elements and with other systems, discovering the way changes in one element or interrelationship affect other elements or interrelationships, testing the system to see how it responds to different inputs and environmental conditions, and modeling the system to understand the parameters and other factors that characterize the system. **Parameters** are numerical variables that define the processes within a system. Another important concept related to systems is "state": the **state** of a system is its status or condition at a given point in time. The range of all possible states of a system is known as its "state space."

It is important to remember what we said about the limitations of analysis: it only drills *down*. A holistic understanding of a system also requires the application of what could be called "systems synthesis" (a rarely seen phrase) and "systems evaluation."

DOI: 10.1057/9781137449320.0008

System dynamics focuses on the ways that systems change over time. A focus on temporality also draws attention to the interactions of systems with each other. This also helps us to understand why some systems are so difficult to change, even when particular elements within the system are changed. Without considering interrelationships of systems with other systems in their environment, we may ignore the ways that other systems work to bring a system back to the way it was.

No matter which approach we use, understanding systems requires that we notice *interrelationships* and *interactions*—that is, communications. Systems thinking reduces our tendency to treat anything as complete in itself, isolated from a larger context. The behaviors and properties of entities are rarely (if ever) produced entirely *within* themselves. If we think behaviors or properties *are* produced *within* an entity, then we may need to rethink the entity in question: perhaps it is a system of its own.

Systems, like all things in the world, are perceived and understood from particular *perspectives*. None of us perceives the world from nowhere; every one of us is *somewhere*, and that shapes how we see. When we define a system's boundaries, we do this from *our* perspective. Because someone gets to make these definitions, systems definitions involve issues of *power* (Williams & Hummelbrunner, 2011). "Who gets to decide" is a fundamental question about any definition of a complex situation. Because of this, we need to resist *totalizing* accounts of systems that shut down other perspectives. Sometimes, systems thinking is used to excessively *systematize* systems, often reducing them to simplistic or mechanistic understandings (Bonnett, 2009). This impulse has operated in schooling for at least 100 years, and its effect is usually not liberating, progressive, or humanizing (Tyack, 1991). *One of the purposes of this book is to offer an antidote to systematization, while championing thinking about schooling in terms of systems.*

Systems thinking is not *inherently* reductive. It shifts our attention from isolated entities to interrelationships—that is, communications—and can help us to reconnect with "natural, mythical, spiritual, and metaphorical ways of knowing by offering an approach to relationship, meaning, and systems that overcomes the limitations of [the] modernist emphasis on quantification, measurement, and certainty" (Fleener, 2005, p. 6). Like Dewey's approach to understanding experience, systems thinking can be a humanizing way to think about schooling, especially when combined with transdisciplinary approaches, as we'll see.[1]

But first, let's look at some general systems types.

DOI: 10.1057/9781137449320.0008

Types

Sometimes, the behavior of a system can be predicted easily, based on a simple understanding of the interrelationships in the system. We can say that such systems are simple. **Simple systems** are often closed; that is, they have no interaction with their environment. A good example of a **closed system** is a battery-powered clock. (I chose a battery-powered clock because one powered by alternating current wouldn't be closed.) The clock has parts that interact with each other. It has a boundary between what's in the clock (the system) and everything else in the world (the environment). But unless someone declares "the clock is a system," and defines its boundary, the clock is just an assemblage of parts in an entire universe of interconnected stuff. This is what I meant above when I said that the definition of a system involves a perspective. As Dewey said, everything in immediate experience is connected to everything else. Only when we start to think about a situation do we start to make distinctions and examine particular relations.

Open systems have interactions with their environment, which either supplies inputs or accepts outputs (or both). A good example is a contemporary automobile. It takes in fuel and oil and oxygen (and maintenance), and it puts out heat and exhaust (and locomotion). The automobile is certainly **complicated**, with more than 20,000 different parts or components. However, the automobile is not *complex*. Its behavior is fairly easy to predict. You step on the gas; it goes. You step on the brake; it stops. Its interactions are *mechanical*: they don't tend to vary much over time.

Complex systems have multiple diverse components or factors that interact in multiple diverse ways, producing diverse outcomes that are difficult to predict (Page, 2010). Complexity in a system means that the system is not mechanical: its parts don't always act in the same way, and the system as a whole doesn't always produce the same output. Complexity is increased by interactive interrelationships, for example, when a change in one element causes a change in another element, or causes a change in the rate of change of another element, or when changes in the processes of the system change the system as a whole. Complexity is also increased by diversity or variation within a system. Complexity characterizes systems which have a "life" of their own, both in the figurative and literal sense. Complexity is complex. (This isn't a completely redundant statement.)

DOI: 10.1057/9781137449320.0008

Several good examples of complex systems are living cells, the brain, a person, a crowd, a city, or a society. A school is a complex system. It involves many diverse interacting parts, and how the system will behave from day to day (or even minute to minute) is hard to predict. Schools input people and things, and they output learning (among other things). Without the external world supplying the "raw material" and accepting the products of a school, the school would cease to exist! But within the system of a school, an internal "logic" of behavior—or culture—may strongly differentiate it from the environment. Such differences between internal and external conditions can be an indication of a system's health, as we'll see.

An excellent metaphor for thinking about complex systems is the idea of an ecology. In biology, this refers to the complex set of interrelationships of living organisms (individually, in groups, as species) with their environment. If we think of Dewey's notion of situation as equivalent to the concept of system, this quote from Boisvert rings true:

> The crops are rooted in the soil, which is aerated by earthworms, insects provide the means of pollination for the plants, rain falls on them, and energy is received from the sun. The interconnections are real.... A genuinely inclusive empirical method does not uncover isolated, discrete entities. Ordinary experience reveals entitles in varied, multifarious forms of interrelationships. (1998a, p. 21)

On this way of thinking, *situations* are systems, and *all thinking is systems thinking.*

Schools have ecologies as well. Think about what happens to a school when its graduates are unable to find suitable work or appropriate higher education: morale drops, the dropout rate goes up, and motivated students leave. This is an example of how the involvement of people brings *time* into a system: current students are looking at current graduates and imagining their own future based on that.

Generic traits of systems

All systems can be understood using a common or generic set of qualities or properties.

Remember the qualities that Dewey identified as the generic traits of existences? Boisvert (1998b) summarized them as interaction, complex-

DOI: 10.1057/9781137449320.0008

ity, temporality, and uniqueness. These traits apply to systems as well. *Systems are existences.*

What else can we say about systems? The qualities I am about to describe come from systems theory, not Dewey's pragmatic naturalism. But the synergies between these two approaches is striking.

All systems have *purposes*—whether they are aware of this or not. Perhaps a better word for purposes that are not conscious is "functions." We can understand a system's functions through a set of questions:

- Does it operate completely within itself or does it interrelate with other systems or entities?
- Does it respond to changes in its environment?
- Does it take "stuff" from that environment (i.e. inputs) and turn it into different stuff (i.e. outputs)?
- Does it moderate or accelerate change in its larger environment?
- Does it convert changes in the environment into another form, such as information or signals that can be measured or interpreted to understand the environment?

All systems have *processes*, which typically involve the interrelationships that a system has both within itself and with the external environment.

- Processes either further a system's functions directly or they support other processes which do.
- Processes sometimes repeat themselves, either maintaining the system or contributing to important system functions. Sometimes, processes even repeat themselves on the same inputs or materials, or on their own outputs.
- A process that repeats itself on the same material can display some very interesting properties and produce very complex or elaborate results. We say that such processes are either *recursive* or *iterative*.
- *Recursion* breaks an input up into smaller and smaller parts, and then once it can process those parts, it acts on those, and then combines the results.
- *Iteration* repeats a process over and over until it's done.
- Both recursion and iteration add to complexity and make prediction difficult.

All systems display *interaction*.

- The elements within a system interact with each other in processes that realize the system's function.

DOI: 10.1057/9781137449320.0008

- Open systems also display interactions with their environment.
- We can think of interactions as a form of communication or signaling of information. Thus, systems can send messages to other systems.
- Interactions with the environment may create tension, because systems cannot control their external environment. Yet external environments change; this sometimes forces systems to change ... or to disintegrate. *The ways that a school's environment affects the internal functioning of the school are poorly understood.*
- When two systems interact, we see them as "interpenetrating" (Waddock, 1998), like Dewey's conception of habits. Systems can interpenetrate into the interpenetrations of other systems. The relation of one system to another *is a system* of interrelationships.

All systems display some degree of *integration*, unity, or cohesiveness in which the behavior and properties of each component contributes to the behavior or properties of the system.

- Integration is never complete, however, or we could never speak of the components of the system. The *system* would act as a single entity. If there is not enough integration, then the system may fall apart, or literally *dis*-integrate.
- We can say that the integration of a system's components creates its *structure.*
- Components *participate* in the structure of the larger system. This isn't necessarily conscious. This requires us to embrace a broader conception of "participation" than generally held.
- Understanding the integration of a system requires mapping the interrelationships. This is a *qualitative* rather than *quantitative* understanding, emphasizing patterns rather than measurements (Capra & Luisi, 2014).

Complex systems display **emergence**, in which the behaviors or properties of the whole are *more than* simply the sum of the behaviors and properties of all of the individual parts.

- A complex system has *emergent* properties when it involves "the interactions of many sub-components or agents, whose actions are in turn enabled and constrained by similarly dynamic contexts" (Davis & Sumara, 2008, p. 34).

DOI: 10.1057/9781137449320.0008

- The more diversity or heterogeneity there is in a system, the more likely it is to generate emergent properties.
- The interrelationships of various parts produce new behaviors and properties. "Collective possibilities [emerge] that are not represented in any of the individual [entities]" (Davis & Simmt 2003, p. 140).
- A simple example of emergence is when a sequence of musical notes produces a lingering harmonic chord. The chord doesn't exist in the individual notes, but emerges from the combination (Capra & Luisi, 2014).
- Other examples of emergent phenomena include thought, consciousness, identity, purpose, consensus, ideology, culture, and community.
- Schools have multiple, diverse entities in diverse interaction, and so produce emergent properties in diverse fecundity. (That is, a LOT!)

Some systems, which are called "complex adaptive systems" (CASs) can be thought of as *alive*.

- CASs contain entities which are able to adapt to changes in the system or in the external environment.
- CASs keep themselves in balance by continually adjusting themselves. The process in which a system regenerates itself is known as "self-organization," or **autopoeisis**.
- This self-organization is an emergent property, in that the ability of the system to keep itself in balance comes from the combination of entities within it (Page, 2010).
- "Built into any social system, its hierarchy, power structure, sanctions, and taboos—are safeguards to protect against or resist radical change" (Edelfelt, 1979, p. 365). "Such self-maintenance can arise and evolve without intentions, plans, or leaders," especially in complex social situations (Davis & Simmt 2003, p. 140).
- By adapting to environments in ways that ensure their survival, systems adapt to environmental change, and therefore *learn*, and through learning, survive.
- Another word for adapting to changes in the environment is "homeostasis." Adaptive systems keep themselves operating within acceptable parameters.
- For example, a cell produces the enzymes, proteins, and lipids that it needs to, thus regenerating itself continually over time.

DOI: 10.1057/9781137449320.0008

- The challenge for all complex adaptive systems is to find a balance between order and chaos, where the system remains flexible and adaptable, but doesn't lose its integrity.
- Life itself emerged from a system of molecules when that system achieved a certain amount of diversity. It crossed a threshold from simple to complex and was able to reproduce itself from inputs available in the environment (Kauffman, 1995). Like other emergent properties, life isn't found in any specific part or place in the system; it is a property of the whole (Capra & Luisi, 2014).
- The Earth itself can be seen as a complex adaptive system, or even a form of life. The "Gaia hypothesis," which conceives of the planet as a life form, was initially treated with great skepticism by scientists; however, from a systems perspective, the Earth is an organism, deserving great respect and understanding (Capra & Luisi, 2014). It is, after all, our only home. This is an example of how viewing things as systems can contribute to a sense of the sacred.

Social systems

Already in this chapter, you can see that thinking about schools as systems has rich and expansive effects on how we see them. Yet we haven't even begun to understand the complexity of schools, which both *contain* multiple systems within them and *also* interact with a wide variety of other systems that are external to them. The overall landscape of schooling in society is incredibly complex.

Schools, like other social systems, maintain themselves despite this complex environment. Studying humans and their social institutions from a systems perspective is particularly revealing, because of the importance of purpose or intentions in understanding individuals and groups. Unlike purely physical systems, living systems exhibit patterns of *choice* and *preferences* which provide *directionality* and *intentionality* to action. Schools, for example, allow new participants as well as other resources and ideas to come in, but these are generally reshaped to fit into the system's existing norms and expectations. This "socialization" into the system occurs without anyone specifically intending for this to happen. People who have been involved in the system for a while come to see these norms as *normal*, even if they seem strange or surprising to the newcomer. Veterans need to be careful not to forget this strangeness, lest they become dismissive of a newcomer's subjective experience of

DOI: 10.1057/9781137449320.0008

initiation and ignore what newcomers might be able to tell them about the system.

We can see a "disconnect" sometimes in organizations that disregard individuality in favor of efficiency and a commodification of human effort.[2] Newcomers who aren't used to these norms may rebel. For example, schools where the curriculum is set in advance or by distant educational authorities may reduce the motivation of learners. Why would we assume that a young person would respond positively to always being told what to do? We need to be careful not to assume that a student who refuses to participate or who acts out in class is herself the source of the problem.

Less rigidly controlled forms of organization may allow for more individual choices, and yet the overall system has predetermined goals. We can call such a system deterministic. Looser forms of organization that allow for diversity of response might be called "purposive," "heuristic," or—at the highest level of individual freedom—"purpose-seeking" organizations (Bánáthy, 1992).

Purpose-seeking organizations consider the intentionality and freedom of each participant as essential: the system's *function* is to realize the ideals and goals of the participants, in addition, perhaps, to overall shared goals. This reminds us of Dewey's conception of democracy as "a society in which the good of each was the good of all and the good of all the good of each" (Westbrook, 1991, 248–249).

Values

Because of the centrality of ideals in complex social systems such as schools, we need to think about what really matters. "Education is at heart a moral practice more than a technological enterprise" (Biesta, 2007, p. 10). Applying systems theory to schooling—and this is why I prefer the phrase "systems theory" to the more commonly seen "systems thinking"—does not force us to ignore moral values or the qualitative aspects of experience. In this respect, systems theory is quite different from more "scientistic" points of view in mainstream science, which tends to disregard values—distinguishing them from "facts." An example of a scientistic point of view is when educational researchers focus on what "works" to produce a predefined goal (like academic achievement), while ignoring the deeper (and more important) question of what it is that we are trying to achieve. A focus on systems theory—on the other hand—can help us to rearticulate and support such values as democracy,

DOI: 10.1057/9781137449320.0008

freedom, and the ultimate value of every human person, and even leave room for the mythic and sacred.

Complexity

Prediction in situations of complexity is difficult primarily because changes in the behavior or state of one component lead to changes in the behavior or state of other components. Even more complex is when changes in one component change *the way that other* components respond to the *changes* of *still other* components. This is what is meant by complex interaction.

We can say that complex situations are not mechanical or deterministic. However, they are also not random or chaotic (Page, 2010). This is important. Think of a spectrum of systems.

- There are some systems that are ordered, predictable, simple, or closed. They are at one end of the spectrum. These systems are too ordered to exhibit more than mechanical properties.
- Other systems are completely random, chaotic, and impossible to predict or control. They are at the other end of the spectrum. These systems never "get it together" well enough to develop emergence.
- In between these two other types of systems are complex systems. They aren't simple, and they aren't random. They are *complex*. We can even say that complex systems *aim* to find the right balance between order and chaos, a balance that makes emergence and aliveness possible (Kauffman, 1995).

This conception relates in an interesting way to Dewey's conception of inquiry. For him, if reality were such that it was pretty simple, there would be little need for inquiry: we would just respond to things in a mechanical way. If reality was too chaotic, inquiry would always have to be done without any useful knowledge or habits from the past: it would be next to impossible. Because reality is a balance of the stable and the precarious, the predictable and the unpredictable—that is, *complex*—inquiry works (Godfrey-Smith, 1998).

Complexity can be found in a variety of phenomena. Examples include groups of animals (like an ant colony or a crowd of people), the global economy, climate change, a body's immune system, the World Wide Web, the challenges of implementing the Common Core,

DOI: 10.1057/9781137449320.0008

and others. In complex systems, outcomes are not simply the result of one factor changing; rather, changes in one part of the system cause changes in other parts of the system. These effects aren't always *linear*; that is, you can't just plug a set of values or measurements into a simple equation to find out what will happen. Instead, outcomes can only be predicted—if at all—using *non-linear* equations. Non-linear interactions or interrelationships can be defined as "not derivable from the summations of the activity of individual components" (Jorg, Davis, Nickmans, 2007, p. 149).

Linear relationships can be modeled on a Cartesian plane as a straight line. All of the various factors that impact a given outcome contribute directly and additively to the slope of the line and where it crosses the x and y axes. A non-linear relationship can't be modeled that way. There may be a factor in the situation that interacts with the changes in another factor in a way that results in the variables no longer being additive, or separate, but mutually implicated. Generally, non-linear relationships involve variables multiplied by themselves or by other variables. (The mathematics of non-linear relationships are very difficult, which is partly why complex systems often seem beyond understanding by members of the general public.)

All this to say: the various ways that the components and subsystems of complex systems interrelate are, well, *complex*.

Level-jumping

Complex systems can be viewed at a variety of levels. For example, a school can be looked at as a whole, by grade level, by classroom, or by individual student. Each individual student can also be looked at from different levels: at the level of atoms, molecules, organelles (structures within cells), cells, tissue, organs, systems (like the nervous system), or the organism as a whole. As we move from one level to another, different kinds of entities emerge (or become visible) and thus are relevant to our understanding.

Another word for "level" is "scale," as in the scale of a map. Zoom in, and it's a small field of view—a small scale, focusing in on just a little bit. Zoom out, and it's a big field of view—a big scale, showing a lot more.[3]

Any system can be looked at from multiple levels or scales. What's visible at a given level or scale depends on what kind of tool or conceptual framework we are using to look at it. So, at the atomic level, we may see electrons jumping from one orbit to another as atoms absorb

DOI: 10.1057/9781137449320.0008

or release energy, or the way that the electrons are shared in chemical bonds between atoms. If we shift to the cellular level, we see and are likely to think about how cell membranes operate to keep the conditions inside the cell optimal for cellular functioning.

The entities at lower levels aren't *irrelevant* at the higher levels: the absorption and release of energy by electrons and the sharing of electrons in chemical bonds, for example, are absolutely *essential* for the functioning of cell membranes. But at the cellular level we pay attention to different entities, like protein molecules. What we pay attention to, as Dewey told us, is determined by the situation.

The thing is, it is impossible to understand or predict the behavior of a system at a *higher* level than what we currently understand. Knowledge of the ways that electrons jump from one orbit to another, for example, is simply not enough for us to understand how a protein molecule works! Similarly, you can't understand the behavior of large groups of people or of whole societies, using only knowledge of electrons or proteins. This is why reduction often results in over-simplication.

What's more, even the *existence* of entities at a higher level is not evident at lower levels. So if you're focused on electrons, you won't perceive the protein molecule of which they are a part. And if you're focused on the workings of the protein molecule, you won't understand that it is operating in the larger context of a human individual who may be part of a group of people. Focus on an individual, and the concept of a group average or norm makes no sense at all.

I want you to understand this. We are *always* limited in our perception by the level at which we perceive! This is similar to what Dewey said about situations: we notice only what is relevant to the situation as we experience it. This is related to selective emphasis. What do you care about? Is it the big picture, or the narrow one?

The thing is, no particular level is more fundamental or real than any other. The level of human everyday experience, for example, isn't the only level that matters or that is real. Complexity and multiple interconnected levels with diverse and varied interaction is what is real (Kozlowska & Hanney, 2002).

Our everyday experience is limited to our own level of being; that is, unless we find a way to level jump. This requires some kind of tool, or instrument (like a microscope or a telescope, or a map or a model, like statistics). Even then, we need a workable theory about the mechanisms at that other level if we hope to understand it. Without familiarity with

DOI: 10.1057/9781137449320.0008

the mechanisms at other levels, the entities, behaviors, and properties at those levels will seem mysterious—even magical.

Because of the need to shift levels to perceive and understand entities, we refer to those entities that we can only see at higher levels as emergent. *Complex systems* display the emergence of entities, behaviors, and properties that were previously unknown or have been profoundly misunderstood.

Unexpected and powerful things emerge from complex systems like schools. Many of us have felt this. We're involved in situations of schooling that get humming along, and a kind of synergy occurs, and all of a sudden we have a different experience, and we know it to be something more than it has been. This happens sometimes with sports and chess teams, and performing arts, and community service projects—but not very often in classrooms.[4] This generation of *something more* by a school is a natural phenomenon; it is emergence, and we need to recognize it. Considering time helps.

Time

Time isn't just an "add-on" to understanding systems. Time makes systems dynamic and adaptive—and interesting. This takes us back to Dewey's identification of temporality as a generic trait. Everything—every system—is an event, with a history.

Time is "a genuine field of novelty, of real and unpredictable increments to existence, a field for experimentation and invention" (Dewey, "Philosophy and Democracy," 1919, MW 11.50). Time introduces the possibility of *change*, and draws attention to trends and tendencies—to teleology. Time adds complexity to any system, because both the past and the future can affect the present. Recall Dewey's conception of *meaning* as potential consequences? Meaning is future-oriented. As we interact with systems, we bring our existing sense of reality with us. Our experience of the past mediates our experience of the present by bringing in the future. Think back to the graph we created earlier of my life. At any given point in time, I am there, at the origin, experiencing entities in my past, present, and future. My awareness isn't limited to the present. My participation in the situation brings the past and future into the present. As conscious human beings, we bring all three—past, present, future—into *every* experience.

I have already briefly mentioned iteration and recursion. These are two ways of using time to produce complex and emergent effects. While

DOI: 10.1057/9781137449320.0008

these processes seem simplistic if we look at them in a moment of time, after a while these processes can produce profound changes in systems at all levels. You can get unexpected things to happen if you do one thing over and over again. *Doing something minor over and over is much more powerful than doing something major once!*

In our schools, the daily routine creates a space for something to be done over and over. Sometimes we ignore the effects of these repetitions because we are focused on what we believe to be big events or major transition points. We ignore the sudden shifts in a system's dynamics that can result from something adding up to more and more until it reaches a "critical mass" and breaks into consciousness. Unfortunately, schools rarely take advantage of the potential this offers.

Visualizing time

We can easily visualize spatial relationships, however, visualizing *time* is much more difficult. We can't *see* the time dimension, so to see it we convert it into spatial configurations. A clock, for example, helps us visualize time as the sweep of the second hand around a circle. A calendar represents the passage of days in little squares, perhaps arranged in rows of seven. Another example is musical notation. The notes on the staff are arranged in a sequence from left to right, and their location (up and down) represents their pitch. The duration, or length, of each note is indicated by its shape. The overlap of multiple notes on a staff indicates harmonies.

We can also visualize the time dimension using graphs, such as those that show trends. A clock, a calendar, musical notation, and graphs: all of these are *models of time*. They can help us to understand complexity.

Messes and wicked problems

Two additional concepts related to complexity will be helpful in understanding schooling: messes and wicked problems.

A "mess" is what Ackoff (1997) calls a system of interrelated complex problems: "A mess is a system of external conditions that produces dissatisfaction" (p. 427). It is rarely the case that a mess can be cleaned up merely by solving the individual problems that make it up. Like the parts of complex systems, the problems that make up a mess are interrelated, often requiring a synthetic or comprehensive approach to clean it up. Some public schools are messes. Typically, this is because the school has no control over its boundary: the problems of the environment are so

DOI: 10.1057/9781137449320.0008

deep that they overrun the school. Or, the level of morale among the teachers or students is such that they commonly refuse to do what is expected of them. In this case, there is no participation of the parts in the whole. Such schools may need radical restructuring.

Wicked problems are even more complex; they are unique, unstructured *systems* of problems that have no real solution, but which present situations which can be improved or ameliorated, but often at the expense of creating new problems. Often, these systems of problems are extremely complex, involving unpredictability and rapidly changing environments, and often involving complex social arrangements (Barnard, 2013; Skaburskis, 2008; Weber & Khademian, 2008). Examples of wicked problems include poverty, climate change, teenage pregnancy, and epidemics such as diabetes and obesity. Wicked problems can be overwhelming, and they never seem to go away.

Wicked problems are intrinsic to the larger environment of schooling. Schools have to deal with them both because they influence what goes on in schools, and because the graduates of schools will have to handle them. Bringing these two forms of interaction together—in curriculum—can help in both situations. In other words, wicked problems present opportunities for students to learn about complexity, while potentially improving their world.

Notes

1 Transdisciplinarity should not be taken to suggest many different disciplines, but rather a unity of perspective that sees systems as entirely embedded in complex contexts (Bateson, 2011).

2 **Commodification** is the reduction of something complex into something simple: in this case, the reduction of human effort to money or some equally crude measure (like a standardized test score).

3 An excellent visualization of the importance of scale in how we see is a film that Charles and Ray Eames made for IBM in 1977, called *Powers of Ten*. See https://www.youtube.com/watch?v=ofKBhvDjuyo&feature=kp.

4 Ted Sizer (1984, 1992) suggested that classrooms can learn something about effective organization by looking at sports and performing arts. In those situations, students work together for the good of the group, and teachers are coaches.

DOI: 10.1057/9781137449320.0008

4
The Complexities of Schooling

Abstract: *An ecological approach to understanding schools is introduced, along with discussion of some of the reasons that the systems involved in schooling are complex. These include diversity and the complexities of humans, of learning, and of contexts. Approaches to leading and managing complex schools are explored, including barriers to change and an effective change process.*

Cunningham, Craig A. *Systems Theory for Pragmatic Schooling: Toward Principles of Democratic Education.* New York: Palgrave Macmillan, 2014.
DOI: 10.1057/9781137449320.0009.

Cremin (1990) wrote:

> Recent assessments...have been seriously flawed by a *failure to understand the extraordinary complexity of education*—a failure to grasp the impossibility of defining a good school apart from its social and intellectual *context*, the impossibility of even comprehending the *processes and effects* of schooling and, in fact, its success and failures apart from their *embedment in a larger ecology* of education that includes what families, television broadcasters, workplaces, and a host of other institutions are contributing at any given time. (p. viii; my emphasis)

How can we avoid these conceptual failures in our understanding of schooling?

When people talk about "school systems," they usually aren't talking about systems in schooling in the sense that I have been here; rather, they are usually talking about a school district, as in "the school system in Chicago is the third largest in the country." School districts *are* systems, but I mean a whole lot more, at many different levels. So I tend to say "systems in schooling" rather than "school systems."

Squire and Reigeluth (2000) write that even when people talk about improving systems in schooling, they often mean just one system: a state or district system, or just one school as a system. The problem with this approach is that each of these systems is nested within and interacting with other systems. To take this into account, they recommend thinking in deeply ecological terms. A system of schooling, they write,

> is a complex social system that can be defined in a number of ways and can be understood only by being viewed from multiple perspectives. Ecological systems thinkers conceptualize human activity systems much as one would ecosystems... [proceeding] with an eye to the relationships between any given system and its superordinate, coordinate, and subordinate systems, for those relationships strongly influence the success of any change effort. (p. 145)

To put this differently, we need to look at schools and their larger ecologies as "living synergistic social system[s]" (Siegrist et al., 2013). Schools are "living" both in the sense that they include living beings, but also because they have a "life" of their own, with all that entails: they live; they are healthy; sometimes they get sick; sometimes they die or are killed as a way of saving money. They are "synergistic" in that the various components and people involved in a school work together (we hope!) to achieve common goals, and are therefore able to do things that no single person by herself could do. They are "social" in the sense that

DOI: 10.1057/9781137449320.0009

multiple people are involved in multiple interrelationships in and around schools.

It is helpful to keep Dewey's list of generic traits in mind. The systems involved in schooling display these traits. Schools and the systems involved are *complex*; they involve diverse *interactions*; they change over *time*; and they are *qualitatively unique*. They also display the generic traits of systems that we discussed in the previous chapter: purposes or functions, processes, interactions, integration, and emergence. And like other complex systems, the systems involved in schooling benefit from diversity and suffer from standardization.

What makes schooling complex?

The typical school is not easily described. Each school is different from every other school because each is made up of different components (and people) and each is related to its own specific environment in complex ways. But there are some common *attributes* of schools: generic traits, if you will. These are worth considering if we want to understand schooling in *general*. Systems thinking can help us structure our examination of such common attributes, by influencing our choices regarding attention and methods of inquiry.

One important insight already mentioned is that systems in schooling are always nested. Thus, understanding schools always requires looking at multiple levels. A short list of the levels within any school would include the individual students, classrooms, grade levels, departments, faculty, and administration. Major subsystems include the attendance system, the schedule, and the curriculum (at various levels). Recall the triangle I introduced earlier, with schooling at one corner, ideology at another, and political economy at the third. This can be used to better understand the relevant environment of a single school as well as systems of schooling. Levels outside the school include the school district, the community, school board, the state board of education, accrediting agencies, the federal department of education, and the global economy, as well as ideological factors such as "the American Dream," evolving attitudes toward equality including meritocracy, conceptions of intelligence and merit, and attitudes toward work and play. This list does not even begin to capture the number of systems and factors involved in a typical school. At any level we could describe interrelationships involving the

DOI: 10.1057/9781137449320.0009

people, the physical spaces, the organizational schemes, the ideas, and various events and processes.

It is easy to get overwhelmed once we begin to list even the most obvious elements. Navigating our way from one level to the next or from one system to the next requires detailed knowledge and experience. This is one of the reasons that schooling is so difficult to understand or to change, despite the continual attempts of outsiders to characterize schooling using simplistic understandings derived from other domains.

Let's examine the complexity of schooling in somewhat more detail.

I will discuss four major reasons or causes for the complexity of schooling: (1) it includes multiple diverse people; (2) each of whom is complex; (3) and whose learning is complex; and (4) the contexts of schooling are complex.

Diverse people "complexify"

The first cause of schooling's complexity is that *schooling always involves multiple diverse people*. For us to call it "schooling" rather than something else, like "self-study," it always involves at least two people. There's at least a teacher (or at least a text) and a student. This is complex in itself, not least because people *always* differ from one another. As a general rule, diversity increases complexity (Page, 2010).

Imagine a one-on-one situation, perhaps a student who is receiving some help from a tutor. We tend to think of a "dyad" like this as a fairly simple situation. And indeed it is, compared to what we'll be discussing in a moment. But sociologists point out that any interaction between two people is fraught with the possibility of disintegration, if expectations or behaviors do not match. This is referred to as the problem of "double contingency", because it involves what Talcott Parsons called a "complementarity of expectations" (Vanderstraeten, 2002). Such complementarity can break down, for example, if the student would rather be outside running around with his friends. The tutor may be able to adjust her actions to take the student's mindset into account (and vice versa), but there is no guarantee. The two people involved will somehow have to figure out their common goals and how they plan to achieve them. This is easier if they already have some basic agreements about purposes, but no matter how much underlying agreement exists, the contingency causes some indeterminacy. This indeterminacy actually creates the very possibility of a fruitful interaction, because if the two people were exactly

DOI: 10.1057/9781137449320.0009

the same there would be no gain to be had from interaction (Vanderstraeten, 2002). It is helpful to think of even this situation as an emergent social system involving all of the generic traits of systems.

Typically, however, schooling involves many more than two people. Think of your typical classroom, with one teacher and a bunch of students. The more students there are in a classroom, the more difficult it is to manage, especially at the lower grades, especially with lower-performing students, and especially if the teacher is using student-centered pedagogy (Watson et al., 2013). For one thing, with bigger classes, there is more likelihood that one or more students will experience difficulty on a given day or with a particular subject.

Every student is different in myriad ways from every other student, in terms of heredity, experiences, perspectives, backgrounds, talents, interests, capacities, and needs. Yet classrooms depend on there being *some* similarities among the students (Davis & Simmt, 2003). With luck, they all speak the same language, have had similar prior experiences of subject matter, or share similar values about education. Such redundancies make it possible for cooperation and communication, and for the underlying empathy between students that can motivate them to help each other. But even in a classroom that appears very homogenous on the surface, each student will bring to school each day a quite different, unique set of experiences. In a very heterogeneous or diverse classroom, the range of such experiences—and possible sources of difficulty with learning—can grow to a point that it is almost unimaginable, and thus unmanageable.

Each classroom each day presents a *situation* that includes many different elements. Classrooms are not entirely under the control of the teacher, so the classic notion that the teacher teaches by manipulating the environment of the student (Johnson, 1967) is more of an ideal than a reality. The teacher *tries* to take control of the environment, but is competing with the other people in the room for that privilege. Getting a large group of young people to pay attention to an adult—especially when the adult is trying to communicate something new or hard to understand—is hard enough. This difficulty is increased when more students are in the room, causing more distractions. Pencils are more likely to drop on the floor; someone is more likely to have to go to the bathroom; the P.A. system is more likely to interrupt learning. These events—as well as intentional acts of deviance or non-conformance—affect the students deeply (Vanderstraeten, 2000).

DOI: 10.1057/9781137449320.0009

But classrooms involve more than just the teacher interacting with each student. Each student must pay attention to the teacher *and* to the other students. This makes for a very complex situation: "Thrust together into classrooms or other settings, humans self-organize—that is, codes of acceptable activity, group hierarchies, and so on emerge" (Davis & Simmt, 2003, p. 149). What's more, "the classroom community can and should be understood as a learner—not a *collection of learners*, but a *collective learning*—with a coherence and evolving identity all its own" (Davis, 2005, p. 87). Indeed, one ecologically informed way to understand the relationship between the individual and the collective in a classroom is that the collective *has to* grasp a new concept or skill before any of the individuals can (Hutchins, 2010).

What's more, much of the learning that occurs in schools is gained through interaction with *peers* (Hogan & Tudge, 1999). *Students learn mostly from each other.* Even if the classroom seems completely traditional, with teacher-centered instruction and compliant students, the students are watching each other, taking cues about how to behave, what to pay attention to, and how to incorporate what is being taught or done into their existing understandings. This happens both inside the classroom and outside. The students interact with each other before and after class, talking with each other about the experience of being in the class. The tone of these conversations affects the students' attitudes during the next class. If the conversations are just negative—for example, about how boring it is to sit through the teacher's lectures—then students are less likely to approach the class with eagerness or curiosity. On the other hand, if the students talk with each other in an excited way about the subject matter of the class—especially if they relate it to their own lives or thoughts outside of school—learning may be reinforced. Usually, students' conversations affect learning in both negative and positive ways all at once. This in itself is complex.

Imagine drawing a map of all of the interactions a given student has within (and outside) a given classroom during the course of a school day. Such a map would be difficult to draw. Now imagine doing it for all of the students in the class! Think about this mathematically. If a classroom consists of just one teacher and one student, then any interactions will be limited to just the transactions between those two. Actually, this isn't entirely correct, because there is likely to be a text or other materials (it could be anything) involved. If we include one text, the teacher, and the student, we have three entities or elements in the situation. We could

DOI: 10.1057/9781137449320.0009

draw this as a triangle. Along one side or edge of the triangle, the student interacts with the text. Along another, the student interacts with the teacher. And on the third edge, the teacher interacts with the text. Thus there are three possible types of interactions.[1] If we add a second student, there are now four elements in the situation, making for six types of interactions. Each additional student adds more potential interactions. By the time you get up to the typical classroom of 23 students, one text, and one teacher, there are 300 possible interactions!

But we also need to consider the mental entities involved as well as the individuals. There are important interactions between a given student's idea and another student's question, or the emergence from dyads or small groups of *new* ideas that then interact with proposed methods or activities, questions about those activities, etc. Encouraging students to offer alternative interpretations of each other's ideas fosters even more interaction and emergence. These interactions foster learning. "Concepts and understandings must be made to stumble across one another" (Davis & Simmt 2003, p. 156). As Davis and Simmt (2003) also point out, it's not actually the ideas that bump into one another, but their representations in spoken and written language. This is one reason that written artifacts are helpful, reminding everyone of important ideas and giving them the opportunity to think about something else while the written reminder remains in play. (This reminds us of how valuable writing is for thinking, even if just one person is involved.)

Now consider that most schools have multiple classrooms! More classrooms in a school means more students and more teachers. The largest high school in the United States has more than 8000 students! Imagine the complexity of mapping all possible types of interactions in *that* school! There are 31,996,000 possible interactions, just among the students! Even the map of teacher-to-teacher interactions would be complex. Now consider the added complexity of schooling when you add in administrators, staff, parents, and community members to the mix.

We can take this even further. When we consider the complexity of schooling, we also need to remember that there are over 132,000 schools in the US, employing over 3.5 million teachers and enrolling more than 54 million students. Many of these schools operate within school districts having multiple schools that interact with each other in all kinds of ways. There are over 16000 school districts in the United States. Each of them contains a degree of complexity that is beyond anyone's capacity to fully understand. (This is why we simplify. More on that below.)

DOI: 10.1057/9781137449320.0009

Each person is complex

The second cause of the complexity of schooling is that individual *people are complex*, almost beyond measure. How complex depends on the level you are looking at. There are almost 7,000,000,000,000,000,000,000,00 0,000 atoms in a typical human body. That's 7 *octillion*. These are organized into about 37,200,000,000,000 cells. Each of these cells functions in *parallel* to keep us alive. This is far more complex than the most complex computer ever created. There are about 260 types of cells (Kauffman, 1995). The complexity of those cells varies, but the typical cell contains thousands of different kinds of micro-structures, each necessary for the cell's functioning. The human brain alone contains more than 100,000,000,000 neurons—the cells that do the actual work of controlling the body, thinking, and remembering. Each of these neurons can communicate with tens, hundreds, or even thousands of other neurons, resulting in more than 100,000,000,000,000 connections in a typical human brain. What's more, each neuron can generate new connections all the time, making it possible for us to learn, and the brain itself can grow new neurons when necessary (even into adulthood; Kyritsis, Kilil & Brand, 2014).

If you thought the map of student-to-student interaction in a typical classroom would be complex, imagine a map of the interactions in a typical brain! As one pair of researchers put it, "The brain is a complex temporally and spatially multiscale structure that gives rise to elaborate molecular, cellular, and neuronal phenomena that together form the physical and biological basis of cognition" (Bassett & Gazzaniga, 2011). From the atomic level on up, these phenomena are complex and not well understood. Describing the specific processes that allow the brain to function is beyond the scope of this book; suffice to say that because the *world* is incredibly complex—at so many levels—our brains have evolved to understand complexity. Networks of neurons and their interconnections—together with the resources of culture and spoken and written language that we learn from our society—are ideal structures for building this understanding.

Different regions of the brain have different functions. These different regions also interact with each other in complex ways. So the complexity is both at the level of individual neurons and at the level of groups of neurons. As Cohen and Stewart (1994) put it, "If our brains were simple enough for us to understand them, we'd be so simple that we couldn't" (p. 8). This complexity can be viewed from both the physical level,

DOI: 10.1057/9781137449320.0009

concentrating on the details of the chemical and electrical interactions, or at the cognitive level, in terms of the operations of the mind.

The complexity of the *physical* brain makes possible the complexity of the *cognitive* mind. "The human mind is unlike any other on this planet, not because of its biology, which is not qualitatively unique [compared to other animals], but because of its ability to generate and assimilate culture. The human mind is thus a 'hybrid' product of biology and culture" (Donald, 2001, p. xiii). Or, as Dewey says, "Mind denotes the whole system of meanings as they are embodied in the workings of organic life.... Mind is contextual" (LW 1.230; see also Varela, Thompson & Rosch, 1991).

Learning is complex

This leads us to the third major cause of schooling's complexity: *learning is complex*. This is true at both the physiological level and at the cognitive level, and not only when it comes to learning complicated procedures or sophisticated theories. Learning even the simplest of things requires complex interaction of the senses, attention, short- and long-term memory, insight, analogical and metaphorical reasoning, emotion, interest, and motivation as well as changes in the chemical and physical structure of the brain, often across multiple regions or functions. Each of these functions depends on the availability of energy and on having other, more basic, needs met (Jensen, 2008). What's more, any specific process of learning involves myriad interactions between psychological activities and changes in the physical and cultural context of the learning; no learning takes place in isolation (Hutchins, 2010).

Even ignoring context for a moment, learning involves both the process by which a fact, idea, procedure, skill, preference or attitude is *retained* (or stored), and some other process by which it is *activated* (or retrieved) at an appropriate time. Learning can either be non-associational—in which an instinctive or natural response to a stimulus increases or decreases over time—or associational—in which a stimulus is associated with a response that does not occur instinctually or naturally.

For learning to be successful, some sort of feedback is required. **Feedback** provides a way for systems to self-regulate. The student needs some way of knowing whether what she has retained or activated is correct. The feedback also typically has a motivational aspect. This can be either positive ("Excellent job on that question, Johnny!") or negative ("If you don't get at least 70%, you'll have to take the quiz again!") This is similar

DOI: 10.1057/9781137449320.0009

to the communication between actions and results that any cybernetic system requires.

As I mentioned above, these various processes typically do not take place simply in the one-on-one interaction of a teacher and a student, but in a complex physical environment and social situation involving multiple people.

Contexts are complex

The fourth and final reason that schooling is complex is because schooling *always* takes place within a complex environment or context. There is no schooling (or anything else) without context. And, often the context makes the schooling more difficult. Take, for example, the context of urban schooling, especially in low income areas. The stresses that students have at home in their families and communities, and the challenges they may face later in life finding suitable employment and paying their bills have enormous and significant consequences for the schooling itself. (Remember that people bring the future into the present through their imagination.)

But even schooling in wealthier communities exists within complex contexts. Students in these communities may face enormous stress caused by their families' expectations. The 2010 documentary *Race to Nowhere* portrays what happens to kids when their lives become over-scheduled with activities designed to differentiate them from everyone else—who are also doing the same to differentiate themselves! School leaders need to provide opportunities for students and their parents to discuss reasonable expectations, and perhaps to redefine success in a way that allows kids to be kids.

Not only are the *external* environments of schools incredibly complex; so, too, are their internal environments. Consider what we said above about the complexity of the interactions in a classroom. From the perspective of any individual learner, the classroom is the *context* of learning. This "context is not merely a place which *contains* the student; the student literally is part of the context" (Davis, Sumara & Kieren, 1996, p. 157). "As the learner learns, the context changes, simply because one of its components changes. Conversely, as the context changes, so does the very identity of the learners" (Davis & Sumara 1997, p. 111). The complexities of these interactions and their impact on each individual (including the teacher) are seldom acknowledged in purely methodological approaches to teaching.

DOI: 10.1057/9781137449320.0009

So, to summarize, schooling is complex because it involves multiple people; each of those people is incredibly complex; learning itself is also complex; and schooling always takes place within an environment or context of complexity.

These complexities present school leaders with complex challenges.

Toward better schools

Traditional modes of school management tend to treat schools mechanistically, as hierarchically organized groupings of formally designed functional units whose overall purpose is to efficiently produce expected outputs: typically defined in terms of standardized test scores. Traditional school managers see themselves primarily as problem-solvers, working through the leaders of their units to tweak processes and to solve problems. These managers ask very pointed but fairly specific questions, such as “How can we increase the amount of time devoted to reading instruction?” or “How can we increase parental involvement?” or “How can we reduce the number of students who are sent to the office for discipline problems?” These may be good questions, but they do not lead to an examination of system fundamentals, and are thus only appropriate if the overall system is deemed to be vibrant and effective. Also, they tend to draw attention to just one part of school at a time, leading to “piecemeal” change (Reigeluth, 2004).

In a period of major transformations in the larger society in which schools operate—such as today—more fundamental questions need to be asked, such as: “How is the transition to a global economy changing the learning that will be important for these students as they move into adulthood?” or “How are our students gaining an understanding of complexity?” or “What is the quality of our students’ relationships with each other and what can we do to improve these relationships?” These questions help us to get at the system as a whole and not just identified problems.

A systems (or “systemic”) approach helps school leaders realize that merely fixing specific problems within the school does not assure that the school achieves overall goals. It moves us from asking “Are we doing things right” to “Are we doing the right things”? Attending to ideals and overall goals (perhaps through mission and vision statements, and strategic planning) is also necessary for this kind of transformational change (Barnard, 2013; Jorg, Davis, & Nickmans, 2007).

DOI: 10.1057/9781137449320.0009

Successful systems transformation in schools requires simultaneous attention to: "(a) vision, (b) [distributed] leadership, (c) school culture, (d) technology planning [, infrastructure,] and support, (e) professional development, (f) curriculum and instructional practices, (g) funding, and (h) partnerships.... Attending to only some parts of the system is not enough to make any real or sustainable change happen" (Levin & Schrum, 2013, pp. 36–37). "Such an approach to improvement is radical, not to mention difficult and risky" (Reigeluth, 2004, p. 242).

Perhaps the most important shift is that schools need to become *learning organizations* (Senge, 1990/2006). Learning organizations continually look at their systems at all levels, including how they think about those systems, considering how system transformation or paradigm shifts may be required instead of just solving individual problems. Learning organizations embrace their own complexity, and involve all participants at all times in improving systems rather than just solving particular problems. The metaphor must shift from a hierarchy to a network or community of interrelationships where power comes from the empowerment of all (Capra & Luisi, 2014). This is the essence of democratic decision-making.

Barriers to improving schools

Schools are hard to change: they have enormous inertia and tend to absorb or assimilate new approaches or structures in order to maintain themselves. "The conservative nature of the system, by the momentum of its own mass,...grinds down even a would-be bold administrative innovator until even he is absorbed into the conservative mass and reflects its conservative behavior" (Coombs, 1968, p. 121). Changes in one component of a school, or of its systems, cause changes in other components. Complexity and variation make such changes hard to predict. "Soft" systems like the school's culture, morale among the teachers, and the admiration or denigration received by excellent students from their peers have enormous impacts, and sometimes the way those systems work becomes apparent only after a plan of action is implemented.

People who work within complex systems will act in such a way as to ensure that their working conditions and environments stay pretty much the same. If an attempt is made to make substantive changes, those who are *not* directly involved in implementation may become barriers to change. Systemic change therefore requires involving all stakeholders in both understanding current approaches and why they need change, and in implementing new systems.

Murgatroyd (2010) identifies several barriers to changing schools: groupthink, accountability regimes, de-professionalization of teachers, top-down change management, risk aversion, role confusion, lack of incentives to change, resources, weak technological infrastructure, and easiest path adaptability (resistance to change in human systems). Stewart, Raskin, and Zielaski (2012) surveyed superintendents, who identified the most important barriers as mandates, federal requirements, lack of funding, and tenure. (Interestingly, these are factors over which superintendents have little control.) There are also some very specific structural barriers to changing schools, related to the factory model discussed above. One perfect example is the division of students into grades on the basis of age. Not only does this ignore the actual diversity in understanding, skill, and maturity of students at different ages, but it also makes it much more difficult for older and younger students to work together in ways that benefit both. These divisions also affect the school culture in innumerable ways, making it much more difficult to form the school as a learning community (Barnard, 2013).

Other barriers to change include the law of unintended consequences, the tragedy of the commons, and the dangers of routine.

Law of unintended consequences

In a situation of multiple, interacting problems (a "mess"), solving one problem will often cause another. This is the "law of unintended consequences." One arena replete with unintended consequences is educational policy. The accountability expectations of the 2001 No Child Left Behind Act, for example, require that each school's test scores *increase* from year to year. One of the consequences—which may be actually intended by some policy makers—is that more and more schools are seen to be "failing" to make "adequate yearly progress" (AYP). Because this applies only to *public* schools, it is the public schools which are seen to be failing. This has the effect of increasing support for charters and vouchers, which gives parents the option to send their children to a school other than the neighborhood public school.

What's more, because schools tend to focus on the content and skills that are used to evaluate them, No Child Left Behind causes many schools to beef up the time they spend on language arts and math

DOI: 10.1057/9781137449320.0009

instruction. This has the effect of reducing time spent on history, science, and the arts. "Yet those neglected subjects are among the most essential ones for imparting reading skill" (Hirsch, 2006, p. 314). Plus, the schools that most tend to ignore the arts, and science, and social studies are the schools that are most worried about their language arts and math test scores. These tend to be schools that aren't doing so well. The children in *those* schools, who tend to be low income and minority kids, get denied the opportunity to learn the subjects that are not tested, exacerbating the existing differences between schools serving different social classes (Anyon, 1997; Ravitch, 2010).

Fink (2003) suggests that the tendency to treat problems in isolation from one another (reductionism) and to consider cause and effect only in a linear way (mechanism) contributes to the tendency to produce unintended consequences. He thinks that policy makers need to be more attuned to the beliefs and intentions of *local* actors in the education arena, which will help them to pay attention to different perspectives and possible outcomes. "It makes sense, then, to keep this aspect of complex systems in mind and to consider not just the primary goal of any given measure, but also its potential effects on other sectors of the system" (Dörner, 1997, p. 21). Ackoff (1997) adds that to avoid having unintended consequences, we should focus on *planning* rather than on problem solving. That is, we should focus on improving systems rather than solving individual problems, and try to understand the system holistically rather than simply focusing on a particular goal. Complexity requires that we *think* more complexly.

One example of more complex thinking is when the external environment of a school is becoming increasingly complex, such as a greater diversity of students in a school district, or diverse community expectations, or multiple mandates from different levels of government. Such a situation should not immediately suggest that the *internal* structures and processes need to become more complex. Increasing the complexity of the systems in the school may solve a temporary problem, but it may make the school less able to respond to new changes and have other unintended effects. A better approach is to focus on giving individuals and groups within the school autonomy, so they can manage the complexity they are facing with more flexibility or agility. While this may seem counter-intuitive, to the extent that management structures can be *devolved or distributed*, the more adaptive and flexible the system will become.

DOI: 10.1057/9781137449320.0009

The tragedy of the commons

The "tragedy of the commons" was first identified by Garrett Hardin (1968), who had been enamored of Adam Smith's idea that markets would produce the best possible outcomes if each individual pursued their own interest. However, Hardin noticed that in some cases, where the "good" that was being utilized for personal benefit was held in common, the net effect of individuals utilizing that good would be that the good would be used up. His iconic example was a "common" field that was used for grazing. Each herdsman would be motivated to add additional cattle or sheep, because they would gain maximal benefit from the additional member of their herd, but only lose a fraction (since the "loss" would be spread among all of the herdsmen).

Smith and Rabin (2013) apply this concept to the accountability movement in an interesting way. Children in public schools, they argue, are a kind of common good. The expansion of standardized testing is a use of this common good. Because the collateral cost of increased standardized testing is not borne by policy makers (but by the individual children), there is a tendency for policy makers to over-utilize this resource, resulting in an overuse of standardized testing. The result is that "we teach them that they are not in school to learn; instead, they are there to perform" (p. 750). Once again, schooling seems designed to produce compliance. Compliant children are less creative and energetic than are children who exhibit uniqueness, and systems that aim for compliance are less intelligent.

The dangers of routine

Bánáthy (1996) provides a somewhat technical but fascinating discussion of the role of information in living systems such as schools. **Information** (as signals for action within the system and as knowledge about the system) can be categorized as "state-referential" or "non-state-referential." "State-referential" means that the information is coded according to an already-known set of "states" or conditions of the system, subsystem, or various components—its "state space."

Consider, for example, the taking of attendance. When the teacher fills out the attendance slip, she marks each pupil as either "present," "not present," or "tardy." These are the "states" that any given student *has to be in* according to the system. There are no other choices.

Now, imagine that some student has developed the ability to be in two places at once. Suppose he could leave his body in the classroom,

DOI: 10.1057/9781137449320.0009

but take his mind elsewhere. (This isn't too hard to imagine, is it? Think about *me* after I misspelled *cliff*.) What would the teacher mark on the attendance slip if the students' body had shown up but his mind had clearly not? If the teacher wanted to accurately account for the student's state, she might mark *both* "present" and "not present." But how would the Attendance Office deal with that? Most likely with some kind of irritated message to the teacher that only one box should be checked for each student!

But suppose for a moment that the presence of the body but the absence of the mind is information that is potentially useful in understanding student academic performance? Shouldn't this be captured somehow? Individuals are able to respond to information that is not state-referential, *if they are attuned to it*. An Attendance Officer who was attuned to the possibility that the attendance system might need to evolve to incorporate new important information might respond differently. But *systems* tend to want information to be predictable.

There are many more examples, both hypothetical and real, in which the information systems used by schools cannot handle information that is—or might be—useful. This is not uncommon in social systems. "When this happens the system in question gets into a rut, it becomes confined to the state space in which the informational processes are defined, it becomes an artifact that has outlived its usefulness" (Bánáthy, 1996, n.p.).

There are some information situations in which state-referential processes are appropriate. Generally, these are those information situations where the information really will *always* conform to a predefined state space, for example, the date or the time that something occurs. We can be fairly certain that the state space of dates and times isn't going to become inadequate for the relevant information. In such cases, we can use computers to make decisions: for example, if a student has been "not present" for 15 days during this academic year, execute a process to signal him and his parents that he may not meet requirements for promotion to the next grade. Automating this process frees people to focus on more important tasks.

But consider as a counter-example information about someone's gender. The emergence of new gender modes in recent years, where some people don't define themselves as either male or female, has led to some difficult situations in schools, especially with the collection of relevant information but also with any automated processes related to gender. Human intervention is necessary to prevent those processes from breaking down in light of the emergence of new information states (Bánáthy, 1996).

Another implication of the fact that a lot of systems in schools rely on "state-referential" information is that these systems are relatively impervious to imposed design changes from school improvement consultants or school reformers. The systems have no way of handling information that doesn't conform to their state space, so the information related to the proposed improvement just "bounces off" the system, which continues functioning as it was before. Schools, like other social systems, are replete with such self-organizing functions, which keep them operating according to routine.

Non-hierarchical management

One common approach to managing complexity in schools is to impose a "command and control model" (Murgatroyd, 2010, p. 260) based on simple measures of effectiveness (such as standardized test scores). This structure is rigid and reductionist, and treats teachers like assembly-line workers, or even as parts in a machine, instead of as knowledge professionals. This reduces their (and their students') creativity as well as their job satisfaction. While some people might like the clarity and routine of this approach, it does not conduce to *learning*, which, after all, ought to be the primary focus of schools.

Is it possible to manage complex systems *without* imposing control? One way to improve on command and control is to involve all stakeholders in the development of "non-negotiable" goals, but then give teachers and other staff autonomy in choosing how to reach those goals (Stewart, Raskin & Zielaski, 2012). Such distributed leadership, where people at all levels of the school are empowered to lead—perhaps in teams (Levin & Schrum, 2013; Spillane, 2006; Stone, 2010)—acknowledges the complexity of schools and their systems and recognizes that the people closest to each situation are in a better position to understand the situation and its nuances, as well as to track the changes in those systems that result from external or internal interactions. It also respects the multiple and unique talents of each person working at the school.

Because schools are complex, and because school leaders often want to increase order and avoid chaos, there is a strong tendency to try to simplify them—both in how we think about them and the actual schools themselves. Some simplification (in thought) is necessary for

DOI: 10.1057/9781137449320.0009

understanding and control. But simplification has the tendency to be reductionist (ignoring important elements) and mechanistic (treating people and groups like machines). Knowing what can be simplified and what can't is important. Most importantly, if we don't take the actual experience of students and teachers seriously, we will tend to believe in simple conceptions of teaching and learning, to *reduce* what matters to stimulus and response (behaviorism), and to treat people as if they *are* their behaviors. This ignores intention, purpose, meaning, creativity, imagination, ideals, and so much of what makes humans wonderful and unique.

Simplifying complexity

Reductionism tries to understand systems by breaking them (in thought) into easier-to-understand subsystems or parts. Hutchins (2010) cites Plato in reminding us that conceptually breaking systems into parts works better if we divide them where the connections and interrelationships are weakest: metaphorically, if we *cut them at the joints*. (This analogy rather unfortunately refers to cutting up a piece of meat.) This principle seems to have motivated Bánáthy to suggest dividing schools into four major subsystems: the learning system, the instructional system, the administrative system, and the governance system (described in Reigeluth, 2004). This seems intuitively sensible because it seems to break up the school into subsystems with distinct functions, but in fact such a division may cause us to ignore many important complex interrelationships.

As we've said, to begin to comprehend schooling, even experts need to simplify things somewhat. In tightly coupled systems, this is very difficult to do. Also, depending on what level or function we are paying attention to, we may divide phenomena that are not currently receiving our attention in ways that will affect later decisions. Put differently, we tend to see what we expect to see, and ignore interrelationships that are (temporarily) under our radar. Generally, it is important to remember Dewey's warning that any conceptual distinctions we make are *in our heads* rather than in reality, which is fundamentally whole.

But some simplification is necessary for understanding. There are three general types of simplifications that work without causing too much reduction—provided we remember that these are simplifications rather than the whole picture: always remember Whitehead's warning to seek simplicity but distrust it!

DOI: 10.1057/9781137449320.0009

1 We can look at the system at a moment in time, as a *still* picture, thus temporarily ignoring change and complex interrelationships but seeing the basic structure.
2 We can look at the system over a period of time, as a *motion* picture, thus temporarily ignoring structures but seeing basic processes.
3 We can look at the system from a *big* picture standpoint (also known as a "bird's eye view"), thus temporarily ignoring details but seeing how the system relates to its environment and to other systems (Bánáthy, 1992).

Notice that each of these simplifications temporarily ignores an aspect or dimension of complexity. Each of these is a type of *model* of what is real.

Any simplification of any system needs to at least pay attention to major inputs, processes, and outputs. For schools as a whole, inputs include people, funding, materials, knowledge, values, and energy. The processes include the development of aims and priorities, content (curriculum), teaching, learning, management, scheduling, facilities maintenance, quality control, finance, and perhaps research (Barnard, 2013; Coombs, 1968). Educated people and waste products, as well jobs for teachers and staff, go out.

This description is quite *linear*. It ignores the possibility of interactions among the inputs or the fact that the processes are inherently messy or that outputs might affect the processes through feedback. But simplification—as long as it is done only conceptually and temporarily, so we avoid the tendency to take our *analysis* or model of a system for the system itself—helps us to see a system's possibilities by focusing on just certain things at a time.[2]

A different way to look at reality that avoids reductionism is "expansionism," which is "aimed at understanding larger and larger wholes in which our systems of interest are embedded" (Bánáthy, 1995, p. 2; see also Ackoff, 1997). Expansionism is *synthetic* as opposed to *analytic*: it looks to context rather than parts, connections with other systems and the environment rather than breaking things into pieces. Expansionism also allows the teleological concepts of function and purpose into explanations, thus moving well beyond mechanistic, reductionist, or deterministic understandings of reality and taking time into account. Finally, expansionism welcomes interdisciplinary approaches to understand the world and to solving problems.

The use of *both* reduction *and* expansion may be the best approach to understanding complex systems. This reminds us of Dewey's sugges-

DOI: 10.1057/9781137449320.0009

tion that inquiry should pay attention to *both* distinctions *and* relations. Moving back and forth between parts and wholes is the essence of a systems approach to inquiry.

The change process

A common principle of approaches to systemic change is that they must involve everyone: all of the people involved must "buy in" to the process and the intended outcomes (Reigeluth, 2004). However, it is unrealistic to expect everyone to share the same vision or goals from the start. A *process* of working toward building shared vision is in a sense more important than implementation of change.

An overall vision for what the school should *do* is the basis for other aspects of the process of improving schools. Idealization is the process by which a compelling vision is generated. It involves a shared process of brainstorming what the school might be like—without considering financial or political constraints (Ackoff, 1997). Temporarily ignoring constraints helps the imagination to flow, to consider possibilities that might otherwise remain hidden. The vision should articulate the assumptions that have guided the design process, be explicit in articulating the values or purposes that the new system should further, and include some understanding of the systems, resources, and relationships that are most important to the functioning of the new system. The more specific the vision can be in describing the system's organization, the more successful the next phase is likely to be.

Using this vision, an ideal system is then designed *on paper* or using modeling software. This design must take into account the primary characteristics described in the vision, as well as four principles for understanding the initial system (Bánáthy, 1995, p. 4):

- **a.** "In open systems there is interaction between the systems and the environment."
- **b.** "The system is separated from its environment by its boundaries; input enters in the system through breaks on the boundaries."
- **c.** "The system's input is transformed into output."
- **d.** "The output of the system is dispatched into the environment."

These four principles help us to visualize or model the system we are dealing with. There are four phases of such modeling. Typically, these

DOI: 10.1057/9781137449320.0009

phases are implemented sequentially, but later phases can also inform the earlier phases:

- First, we need to analyze the system and understand its *boundaries*, the *environment*, what counts as *input*, and what counts as *output*.
- Next, we need to come to a better understanding of the *interrelationships* exhibited by the system and its environment.
- Then, we need to understand the *structure* of the system at a given point in time ("freeze frame") and how its various components operate together to transform the inputs into the outputs.
- Finally, we can try to understand the system *dynamics*, of how it changes or operates over time.

Using these steps, we design a model of the system using appropriate tools.[3]

Then, a plan for implementation can be developed. "The essence of planning is to think through the consequences of certain actions and see whether those actions will bring us closer to our desired goal" (Dörner, 1997, pp. 153–154). A **plan** is a chain of (inter)actions designed to lead toward a goal. Sophisticated planning requires more than action steps. For each action, we must specify what conditions would cause us to take that action, and also what result the action is intended to bring about. Merely planning a set of actions is easier, but it is more likely to lead to undesirable results.

Planning can be done in two directions. *Forward* planning takes us from where we are to where we want to go; *backward* (or "reverse") planning takes us from where we want to go back to where we are. Educators are familiar with backwards planning through the concept of backwards design, which is used in developing curriculum. In the curriculum approach, desired outcomes or objectives are identified first, followed by the development of good assessments for these outcomes, followed only then by development of the learning activities that are necessary for helping students do well on those assessments (Wiggins & McTighe, 2005). Sometimes the right approach to planning requires both forward and backward planning processes: we build a "bridge" (so to speak) from both ends, meeting somewhere in the middle.

Participants should resist the temptation to alter the characteristics of the system from what are described in the vision as they wrestle with

DOI: 10.1057/9781137449320.0009

the feasibility of implementation. Creating schedules that include the assignment and sharing of responsibilities, perhaps implementing the new systems a piece at a time, or with a small sample or subset of the eventual implementation goal (i.e. through a pilot project), is part of the plan for implementation (Ackoff, 1997).

All of the types or levels of *interaction* that a system might have with its environment need to be considered. Bánáthy and Jenks (1990) categorize these as *information exchange* (the simplest and least complex form of relationship in which signals are sent from one system or component to another, and perhaps back again); *cooperation* (in which different systems or organizations share common goals and sometimes work together on those goals, but remain autonomous); *coordination*, where activities are no longer the responsibility of a particular system or organization but such responsibilities are shared; and *integration*, where schools and other organizations consciously reconfigure themselves to optimally utilize and share resources and for the benefit of an entire community. Integrative approaches to community problems apply multiple disciplines and holistic approaches to understand interpenetrating systems that might be too complex to untangle from any one discipline (Waddock, 1998).

Notes

1 This approach—counting the number of possible interactions in a classroom—is a very crude measure of complexity. "Measurement should take into account not only the [interactions] themselves but also their nature" (Dörner, 1997, p. 39).

2 "Any model abstracts, and focuses on some particular set of properties at the expenses of others. If the theorist tried to build into their model every parameter they believed plays some role, the model would almost always be uselessly complex" (Godfrey-Smith, 1998, p. 51).

3 Choosing the right *tool* for the modeling can help understand the system better. The simplest form of model might just be a *list*, for example of the key components we see in the environment and within the system. A more complex model might use concept mapping software to map the interrelationships among those components. Use of a systems modeling software like *InsightMaker* (http://insightmaker.com/) or *Stella* (http://www.iseesystems.com/softwares/Education/StellaSoftware.aspx) allows more sophisticated mapping of relationships among components, including the use of quantitative data and equations to model interactions.

DOI: 10.1057/9781137449320.0009

5
Learners and Learning

Abstract: *The complexities of learners and of learning are explored in greater detail using Bronfenbrenner's Ecological Systems Theory and other concepts from systems theory. Diversity is examined closely, with attention to Aristotle's eudaimonistic conception of what it means to develop as a person, with additional ideas from Dewey. The concept of unique potential is offered to help understand and to value individual variations among students.*

Cunningham, Craig A. *Systems Theory for Pragmatic Schooling: Toward Principles of Democratic Education.* New York: Palgrave Macmillan, 2014.
DOI: 10.1057/9781137449320.0010.

One way to think about any individual is in terms of the many systems of which they are a part. We can see a complete person as a system. This would be a "complex adaptive system," with all that entails. We can also think of them as containing, or being made up of, systems such as motivational systems, emotional systems, and learning systems, or we can see them as involved in situations containing many overlapping or interpenetrating systems (Waddock, 1998). Given what we've learned so far about systems, we would also expect learners to be involved in interaction (situated, or in a context), to be complex, to have a temporal dimension, and to be qualitatively unique.

While "no mechanically exact science of the individual is possible [since] an individual is a history unique in character" (Dewey, *The Quest for Certainty*, LW 4.199), having a good understanding of the generic traits of humans—as learners and as teachers—is fundamentally important for understanding schooling.

Ecological systems theory

Urie Bronfenbrenner's *Ecological Systems Theory* sees the growing human being as living in a series of contexts which are themselves embedded within larger contexts: nested systems within nested systems. Bronfenbrenner was a critic of more mainstream approaches to human development, which tended to examine isolated influences on development. As with other applications of systems theory that we have discussed in this book, systems draw attention to interrelationships. It is those interrelationships that most directly affect a child's development. Bronfenbrenner's theory also serves as an excellent example of how systems theory can provide conceptual tools for understanding complexity.

Bronfenbrenner (1979) identified five concentric circles around each person, which he called the micro-, meso-, exo-, macro-, and chronosystems. Microsystems are the immediate contexts of the child's life, including the family, peer group, classroom, and church. The ways that these microsystems interact with one another is the mesosystem. It is in the micro and mesosystems that the child spends her time; the larger systems primarily influence the child through their effects on that context. The exosystem is the larger contexts of the mesosystem, such as the parents' employment situation, policies of the school district, the schooling a teacher has and continues to receive, and the influence of mass media.

DOI: 10.1057/9781137449320.0010

The macrosystem is the larger contexts of the mesosytem, including the culture, national policies, economic patterns, and social conditions. The macrosystem also includes the controlling systems of ideas, or ideologies of the society. The chronosystem cuts across all of these other systems, and includes the ways that time includes all of the systems. (Dividing time out in this way reminds us of the types of simplifications discussed above, one of which involves temporarily ignoring time.)

These ever-widening circles relate to the discussion above about levels. It also helps us understand the "boundless" nature of systems such as human beings: because every level is affected either directly or indirectly by every other level; literally "no man is an island." This makes things messy when it comes to understanding biological, conscious, cultural beings such as human beings and in teasing out the factors involved in their development, but such is the nature of complexity.

A child's development is most directly affected by the specific ongoing experiences (known as "proximal processes") that the child has with people and objects in her immediate settings—*not* the isolated attributes of those settings such as low income or race. (Such attributes are useful for making only statistical predictions—predictions that are wrong as much as they are right.) That is, an understanding of the child requires paying attention to her own actual experiences: thus, Bronfenbrenner utilized a **phenomenological** approach to understanding children—that is, understanding their experiences from *their* perspective.

If the people in the different settings experienced by the child (for example, the family and the school) have ongoing and detailed communications about her particular experiences and share expectations—and to the extent that her transitions between these different settings are smooth and seamless—the more reinforcing these contexts will be and the more significant for the child's development.

Later in life, Bronfenbrenner expanded his Ecological Systems Theory by drawing attention to the important role that a child's *biology*—that is, her genetics—plays in development. His Bio-Ecological Model emphasized that the relationship of an individual's biology with her environment is a bidirectional one: the environment affects the biology of the individual (especially her genetic expression, or phenotype) as much as the biological development affects her interactions with the environment (Bronfenbrenner & Ceci, 1994). This kind of back-and-forth interaction is typical of complexity. Paying attention to back-and-forth interaction is critical for understanding human development—and learning.

DOI: 10.1057/9781137449320.0010

The complexity of learning

All learning takes place in an environment or context. The contexts of learning can be viewed as a learning ecology, or, as Bateson (2000) put it, an "ecology of mind."

"A fuller understanding of the phenomenon of learning must embrace the dynamic and complex interplay of individual and environment, refusing to separate knowledge from action, refusing to forget the body" (Davis, Sumara & Keiren, 1996, p. 155). One cannot really understand learning unless one is willing to adopt multiple disciplinary lenses, such as neurophysics, neurobiology, developmental psychology, cognitive psychology, learning sciences, sociology, and more (Jensen, 2008; Waddock, 1998).

Intelligence can be defined in terms of systems. Flexibility of intelligence is a result of incorporating a variety of perspectives. Intelligence is

> ...the capacity of a system to respond not just appropriately, but innovatively to novel circumstances. The extent of a system's intelligence is linked to its range of possible innovations, which in turn is rooted in the diversity represented by its agents. A system's range of possibilities—its intelligence—is thus dependent on, but not necessarily determined by, the variation among and the mutability of its parts. (Davis & Simmt 2003, p. 148)

Schools incorporate this insight to some extent in the way that they bring people with a variety of specializations (case management, social work, special education, psychology, nursing, occupational therapy, parents, and sometimes the student) together to manage special education cases. If case management teams work well, these teams are likely to apply an interdisciplinary perspective (and not simply multiple disciplines in parallel) to each case. In some cases, where students face multiple challenges, their situations can even be seen (not explicitly!) as "messes" or "wicked problems" (Waddock, 1998). This multidisciplinary approach should be applied to developing individualized learning plans for *all* students, not just those with defined special needs. It can also be used to inform the *goals* of learning. We'll return to that, later.

Thinking of the learner as a learning system helps to understand the complexity of learning. Bronfenbrenner (1979) defined learning as a "person's evolving conception of the ecological environment and his relation to it, as well as the person's growing capacity to discover, sustain, or alter its properties" (p. 9). As we know, children (and even adults) are

DOI: 10.1057/9781137449320.0010

changing all the time, while preserving the identity of the overall system. These changes are often improvements (although there are certainly situations where people develop in ways that are not positive—for example if they develop an aversion to math from things that happen in math class or while doing their homework). What makes those improvements possible is the fact that the learner—as a living system—is constantly replicating itself, but in such a way that the replications aren't *exact*, but incorporate adaptations to (functional *information* gleaned from) ongoing experience. The capacity to replicate (which is fundamental to living systems) is also the capacity to *evolve* over time: to *learn*.

As Dewey and others have pointed out, the *teacher* doesn't cause learning to occur directly. Instead, the teacher modifies the learning environment to scaffold a desired change in the learner(s). The word "scaffold" is a good one, because it captures the fact that the scaffolding or learning supports are *outside* of the learner-as-learning-system. The scaffolds help the learner to respond to the learning environment appropriately, perhaps by reducing the cognitive load of a new learning activity. If a learning activity makes a difference for the student—and it should—it might be upsetting to something he currently believes, either about himself, or about the world. This upsetting aspect of learning cannot be avoided, unless the activities of the classroom are so benign as to make no emotional difference to the students.

Biesta (2007) points out that learning is not a mechanistic process, because it inevitably involves an interpretation or "use" of experiences by the learner, thus personalizing the outcome, or at least making a personal decision as to how to respond. It is thus an *interaction* (or "transaction," to use Dewey's term) and *never* simply a passive taking-in by the learner of what the teacher says or does.

Working toward an understanding of the situatedness of learning, and the ways that relations between learner(s) and teacher(s) shape learning, helps us to understand also the role of culture in learning, as well as its overall complexity. "Teaching tends not to be regarded in its original and irreducible complexity. It is our contention that until it is we will continue the ineffective and potentially damaging practice of regarding learners as isolated, detemporalized, and decontextualized subjects" (Davis & Sumara 1997, p. 121). Davis and colleagues question two "pervasive—and we believe troublesome—'assumptions' [that] seem to be universally enacted in schools: first, that we are able to identify the skills and knowledge that learners will need to become full participants in society and, second, that

DOI: 10.1057/9781137449320.0010

learning is controllable" (Davis, Sumara & Kieren, 1996, pp. 152–153). They believe it is "necessary to look more carefully at the dynamic, ever-evolving fabric of social experience and cognitive action which co-emerges within particular events in the curriculum" (p. 153).

We need an alternative understanding of curriculum as an emergent space for making meaning, rather than conforming to a pre-specified set of meanings (Fleener, 2005). "Such notions as controlling learners and achieving pre-set outcomes must be set aside in favor of more holistic, all-at-once co-emergent curricula that are as much defined by circumstance, serendipity, and happenstance as they are by predetermined learning outcomes" (Davis & Sumara 1997, p. 122; see also Lehmann-Rommel, 2000). This is not to say that curriculum and its enduring traditions ought to be removed entirely from schooling—such would likely be a recipe for meaninglessness rather than freedom, but that it shouldn't be a rigid sequence of topics that precludes shifts in emphasis or direction in response to the questions and concerns of a particular group of students. "There is no such thing as a fixed and final set of objectives, even for the time being or temporarily. Each day of teaching ought to enable a teacher to revise and better in some respect the objectives aimed at in previous work" (Dewey, *The Sources of a Science of Education*, 1929, LW 5.38–39).

One alternative conception of curriculum says that it is "anywhere learning occurs" (Stone, 2010, p. 35). In this conception, curriculum is at least partially emergent (Bonnett, 2009).

Diversity

Diversity is a property of groups; an individual cannot be diverse (Page, 2010). However, an individual can be *unique*, and all human individuals are—meaning that any group of individuals (even two) will contain diversity.

As Dewey believed, "a plurality of diverse interacting and changing existences" (MW 8.7) adds richness to any cultural enterprise—or indeed any complex system. To attempt to reduce diversity starves our culture of its vitality.

Becoming a person

Reductionist thinking tended to exclude any discussion of purpose or goals from understanding cause and effect. This exclusion made sense

DOI: 10.1057/9781137449320.0010

given the mechanistic assumptions of reductionism, but also resulted in separating the realm of human purposes and intentions (that is, teleology) from the realm of science. Dewey's identification of "possibility" as a real factor in real situations can be applied to any situation involving any entity: most appropriately, to human beings. This view serves as a strong corrective to the mechanistic view.

The concept of proximal processes in Bronfenbrenner's later Bio-Ecological Model suggests that a person's unique potential is almost infinitely malleable through sustained attention to particular pathways of development. To the extent that schools—and the larger context of educational policies—can provide the resources for and prioritize such pathways—they could have a profound effect on not only individuals but on groups or even humans as a whole. It is also important to realize that the possibility of profound effects on the development of some individuals in this way contributes to the amazing pluralism and diversity of human development (Bowers, 2012). Focusing on the possibilities of individuals offers an alternative to seeing individual students as merely raw material to be shaped to standards.

Zhao (2012) writes of a "pedagogy of becoming," in which through coming to terms with ourselves and others, we go "beyond who we already are" (p. 673)—not toward some end that has been predetermined (by a totalizing philosophy of what it means to be human or by curriculum developers)—but towards an unknown future self. To define this unknown future in terms of a statistical *norm* or *standard* is to deny the individuality and possibility in each person. The lack of a predetermining of this is an emancipatory ignorance or space of open possibility that leaves room for the child's growth to take place. This space demands a confrontation with one's self, as to who one wants to be (Taylor, 1989).

As adults, it is our responsibility to help students "to struggle to be, to emerge, to gather, and to presence" (Zhao, 2012, p. 674). One of the ways we do this is by helping them to visualize their own "best possibility" (Garrison, 1995, p. 408), and then create situations that help them to realize their best selves. This requires a willingness to help students create "the morally possible [that is] beyond the actual situation" (p. 416).

Aristotle's view of the good life

Aristotle devoted considerable attention to the question of the best possibilities of human beings. His answer focused on what he saw as the function that makes humans different from other forms of life. The purpose

DOI: 10.1057/9781137449320.0010

couldn't simply be living, for that is a function shared by all forms of life, including plants; and it couldn't simply be fulfilling the desires of appetite, for that is shared with the animals. For Aristotle, the purpose of a human being had something to do with the essential function that (to his mind) applies *only* to humans.

For Aristotle, this essential function was the ultimate in human activity: rational thought, or contemplation. But merely thinking rationally wasn't enough of a human end for Aristotle. In his typical fashion, he believed that highest purpose of human life shouldn't be just rational thought that resulted in no change; rather, it must be rational thought directed toward excellence (or *arête*, in Ancient Greek). It is the excellent functioning (or acting) that should be the outcome of rational thought. To Aristotle, this meant a life of *virtue*, which he considered doing the right things for the right reasons at the right time and with the right motivations. The form of thought that results in virtue is rational thought that involves a choice: deliberative thought that results in right choices.

Aristotle provided guidance as to how to make such choices in *Nicomachean Ethics* (330 BC/1962). For any decision, say between two options, a person will find themselves drawn by natural tendency toward one of the options. This natural tendency should be taken as a warning not to allow oneself to habitually choose the personally easier option: otherwise, one is in danger of acquiring a bad habit, or vice. Rather than allowing such a bad habit to form, we should strive to always choose the *mean* relative to us, that is, the mean or average of the two options that takes into account our not-always wise personal predilections. Aristotle referred to this as the "Golden Mean." Thus, someone who tends to overindulge in sweets should cultivate habits of self-control; someone who tends not to have any fun ought to allow himself to look for options that allow for play or enjoyment. A person who tends to avoid physical challenges should find opportunities to expand their comfort zone, while a person who tends to take too many physical risks may need to cultivate a better sense of caution or boundaries. The use of the Golden Mean is a type of cybernetic system moving toward virtue.

The outcome that would emerge from a life of virtuous choices Aristotle called "happiness," or the Ancient Greek word, "eudaimonia." (The opposite of this feeling, "dysdaimonia" might accompany bad or vicious choices.) A better understanding of this word, *eudaimonia*, results from looking at its etymology: eu-daimon-ia, or a state of being in harmony with one's *daimon*, which can be translated as one's soul, one's better self,

DOI: 10.1057/9781137449320.0010

or highest self. I prefer to translate the daimon as one's unique potential for excellence. This may seem circular, since Aristotle was saying that this was the outcome of a virtuous life, which seems to imply a life lived in harmony with one's (unique) potential for excellence, but such circularity is actually an indication that the concept of a unique potential is something that emerges only over time as one seeks the pursuit of excellence.

David Norton did more than any other person to draw attention to the roots and utility of the concept of unique potential. His book *Personal Destinies* (1976) was devoted to the topic, as were several of his later writings. For a eudaimonist, the "daimon" refers to an ideal of perfection, "affording to the actual person his supreme aim and establishing the principle by which the actual person can grow in identity, worth, and being" (Norton 1976, p. 14). For Norton, the potential self is connected to the actual person by a "path of implications, whose progressive explication constitutes... the person's 'destiny'" (Norton 1976, p. 16).

Looking at the etymology of *education* we see that it is a process of "drawing out." What is drawn out? We could say that it is this higher self, or unique potential for excellence (Scheffler, 1985). According to this view, the teacher has a particular role in helping the student see her own potential, both by pointing out when the student's participation is exemplary and helping the student to create a personal vision of his own possibilities. "Eudaimonistic" teaching requires that the student be able to apply his own values to decisions about which aspects of his range of potentials is worth developing, rather than the teacher's values, although teachers certainly play a role in helping to shape the students' values, so we can say there is a recursive or iterative relationship between the teacher's and students' values (Cunningham, 2011).

Dewey's conception of unique potential

The concept of unique potential fits well within the pragmatic, naturalist metaphysics developed by Dewey, who wrote, "To find out what one is fitted to do and to secure an opportunity to do it is the key to happiness" (Dewey, *Democracy and Education*, 1916, MW 9.318). For him, "potentials" are a legitimate aspect of empirical reality. They operate in the realm of meaning, and connect ideals with reality and the future with the present (Cunningham, 1994). The concept also draws attention to the ways that individuals are involved in interrelationships and interactions, are complex, have a temporal dimension, and exhibit uniqueness.

DOI: 10.1057/9781137449320.0010

Above, we discussed the importance of habit in Dewey's conception of the self. But there's more to the self than habits. Within the self, there are both organized, repetitive aspects and unorganized, unactualized possibilities. The organized or "habitual" self represents "those factors of the self which have become so definitely organized into set habits that they take care of themselves" (*Ethics*, 1908, MW 5.326). What allows the self to grow beyond this habitual self are the possibilities, "presented in aspirations which, since they are not yet formed into habits, have no organized hold upon the self and which can get organized into habitual tendencies and interests only by a more or less painful and difficult reconstruction of the habitual self" (p. 326). The set of these possibilities, or aspired-to capacities, represents Dewey's naturalized ideal self.

I want to draw attention to the notion of *expansive ideals*, which don't seek to make things realistic *per se* but seek to motivate a better world. Rockefeller (1991) writes of Dewey's conception of ideals:

> Ideals exist in nature as possibilities rather than actualities. Ideals are possibilities resident in natural events. Such possibilities become ideals when they are apprehended by human intelligence and projected by the human imagination as desired objectives and guides to action. In short, nature is full of ideal possibilities. (p. 396)

Revealed through the application of intelligence to experience, ideals provide the individual with concrete ends-in-view which infuse life with meaning and value. Dewey recognizes that a person, like other existences, has at any time a set of unexplored possibilities that can be realized only through interaction with other entities:

> Since individuality is a distinctive way of feeling the impacts of the world and of showing a preferential bias in response to these impacts, it develops into shape and form only through interaction with actual conditions; it is no more complete in itself than is a painter's tube of paint without relation to a canvas. (*Individualism, Old and* New, 1929, LW 5.121)

And out of interaction the self is formed.

> Individuality itself is originally a potentiality and is realized only in interaction with surrounding conditions. In this process of intercourse, native capacities, which contain an element of uniqueness, are transformed and become a self. Moreover, through resistances encountered, the nature of the self is discovered. *The self is both formed and brought to consciousness through interaction with environment.* ... [T]he self is created in the creation of objects, a creation that demands active adaptation to external materials, including a

DOI: 10.1057/9781137449320.0010

> modification of the self so as to utilize and thereby overcome external necessities by incorporating them in an individual vision and expression. (*Art as Experience*, 1934, LW 10.286–287; my emphasis)

The importance of interacting with surrounding conditions for the formation of individuality is a central aspect of Dewey's later conception of education. "A person's 'potentialities' cannot be *known* till *after* the interactions have occurred. There are at a given time unactualized potentialities in an individual because and in as far as there are in existence other things with which it has not yet interacted" ("Time and Individuality," 1939, LW 14.109). Further, "potentialities are not fixed and intrinsic, but are a matter of an indefinite range of interactions in which an individual may engage" (p. 110). It is also important to acknowledge—and Dewey does—that some of a person's possibilities may be incompatible with other possibilities, and that some discrimination must be made between potentialities which are valuable and those which may be less so (Scheffler, 1985). Such discrimination is a form of evaluative thinking, which we discussed above. Dewey also affirms that individual humans are unique, and that their value cannot be compared to the value of any other person: all such persons are of immeasurable worth, and each of them is incomparable. Another word for immeasurable and incomparable, I suggest, is *sacred*.

Understanding a person's unique potential requires an openness to the full range of possibilities that exist for any person at any point in time. One's own sense of one's own possibilities may be overly limited, based on self-doubt, learned helplessness, and wounds from experiences that one considers—or that others consider—to have been a failure. Hence, all people—especially young people—need advocates who are not so willing to accept the limits of one's own self-image (Noddings, 1988). This could be a parent, teacher, mentor, or other person who is familiar with one's personality, character, and history—but not too familiar, for sometimes such a person needs to be a critic who is willing to push the person well beyond where they are naturally willing to go.

Adolescents develop the capacity to move from a concrete description of themselves based on fairly superficial attributes (the color of their hair or eyes, how tall they are) to understanding themselves as capable of action and of embodying possibilities that can be realized through their actions. This is part of their identity development (Hacker, 1994), and it should be taken seriously by schools, which can use the opportunity of these emerging ways of thinking to help students see themselves in

DOI: 10.1057/9781137449320.0010

terms of unique potential, to understand that "identity [is] a network of contingent relations" (Lehmann-Rommel, 2000, p. 190).

Thus the development of imagination is a proper goal of education. As Dewey wrote, "imagination of ideal ends pertinent to actual conditions is the fruition of a disciplined mind" (*A Common Faith*, 1934, LW 9.35). Imagination of ideal ends pertinent to the ever-changing actual conditions of each person's life is the chief avenue by which persons develop the normative content to a well-lived life. These ideals—as unique potentials—then become the most important tool for the process of moral education.

Variation in classrooms

Biesta (2001) suggests that there *is no possibility* of being who *we are* without others who are different from ourselves. If there were no others who were different than us, we could not *do* anything meaningful. What's more, we cannot *become who we are* without diverse others. Diversity is thus *necessary* for education.

> Since individual freedom and individual autonomy are fostered in societal communication, it seems paradoxical to continue to insist on conformity or consensus. Nonconformance offers the best chance to present oneself as an individualized individual. (Vanderstraeten, 2000, p. 15)

Nonconformance ("opting out") may be positive (new ideas, new styles, innovation of all forms) or negative (reactive, personally destructive). Communicating the intention of an act creates the possibility of refusing to comply with its intention. In other words, it provides the student/recipient of the communication with the freedom to reject it.

Vanderstraeten (2000) discusses some of the work of Niklas Luhmann, who applied systems theory to social systems, including education. Luhmann distinguished between social systems, which use communication as the signals of self-production (*autopoeisis*), and psychic systems (minds), which use thought or consciousness for the same purpose. The differences between these two types of systems are particularly interesting because schooling can be considered a social system that is designed to create changes in psychic systems. This disconnect creates the possibility of non-compliance, or deviance. Rather than treating this as the problem, seeing the expectation that all students are the same as a deeper problem can help schools become more appropriate for all.

DOI: 10.1057/9781137449320.0010

Because of the desire to simplify the processes of schooling, schools tend to treat the unique individuals who attend as students as easily categorized (in terms of age, mostly), and strive for "equal" treatment, which often means treating everyone the same. They also expect compliance from everyone and attempt to reduce the variation of children's values and behaviors. These expectations are a major cause of disconnects that open up between students and school, because, as we've seen, there is considerable variation in classrooms. Not treating everyone the same results in a better fit, and better results. Just to pick one obvious example of variation: students learn at different rates. We cannot continue to expect a whole class of students to "plow through" the curriculum relentlessly and uniformly.

Grouping students by age causes other problems, mentioned above. Barnard (2013) has shown that even a simple readjustment of a school's structure away from age-grading can have big benefits for a school. He advocates having mixed-age groups in homerooms, with students coming into a homeroom at the beginning of their years at a school and staying in that same homeroom until the end, with new students entering the homeroom as others graduate to their next school. Having these mixed-age groups meet every day—even for just ten minutes or however long the homeroom period is—can help a school to become a more close-knit community and help build stronger relationships between parents or other caregivers and the school. This is a perfect example of transformative change: not just solving a given problem, but reimagining purposes and not limiting new visions to what has been done before.

Let me introduce another way of thinking about the diversity of a group of unique individuals. If each person's potential is indeed unique (and I don't think anyone can argue persuasively otherwise), then each person offers something special to a classroom, school, community, or any group (including the larger society). If we reduce uniqueness through rigid standards or expectations of compliance and conformity, we lose possibilities for the future that we may not even realize we are losing. Preserving possibilities, it seems to me, is one way of increasing the odds that we will be able to effectively respond to whatever happens in the future. This applies to any system, including natural ecologies.

In science, the concept of "potential" has a somewhat different connotation than I have been using so far in this book. A potential is a difference or gradient between two entities or systems (Kauffman, 1995). This difference can be utilized to do work.

DOI: 10.1057/9781137449320.0010

In physics, for example, potential energy is energy that can be released because an object is in a different position from a lower energy position. Consider a snowboarder at the top of a hill. Because of gravity and the difference in being at the top versus being at the bottom of the hill, the snowboarder has potential energy, which can be used to do work: to move from the top of the hill to the bottom. Once she's at the bottom, she no longer has access to that energy; there no longer is a *difference* in height. To get that energy back, she has to regain the difference by climbing back up (or taking a ski lift).

Another example is in electricity. A battery is able to run a cell phone because of the potential for electrons to flow from one terminal of the battery to the other. The reason this works is because of a *difference* in electromotive force (voltage) between the two terminals. Once this difference is gone, the battery is considered "dead" and has to be recharged.

In biology, potentials exist across cell membranes. These potentials provide energy for the cell to do its work. By maintaining a higher sodium content inside the cell compared to outside (another difference), the cell is able to acquire additional water. The pressure this creates in the cell—known as osmotic pressure—helps it maintain its shape and avoid being crushed.

In each of these examples, energy is *dissipated* in the process of doing work. If the energy can be replenished, more work can be done. If that work is applied to maintaining the system (as in the example of the cell), we can refer to that as a *dissipative system* (Nicolis & Prigogine, 1977).

I suggest that the concept of potential as difference applies also to human beings and to social systems like schools. The differences between two people is what makes their interaction potentially powerful. The differences between the internal conditions of a school and the external conditions of the larger society is the basis of the school's capacity to influence the society. Similarly, the differences between an introductory course in algebra and a more advanced course is why students will gain additional learning in the more advanced course.

Eliminate differences (potentials) and you eliminate possibilities.

In short, *diversity* makes the world go round.

DOI: 10.1057/9781137449320.0010

6
Teachers and Teaching

Abstract: *The complexities of teaching, teachers, and of teacher education are explored using some of the concepts previously introduced together with the important role of intersubjectivity and caring in classrooms. School leaders need to trust teachers and provide them with professional autonomy to allow their own unique potentials to flourish.*

Cunningham, Craig A. *Systems Theory for Pragmatic Schooling: Toward Principles of Democratic Education.* New York: Palgrave Macmillan, 2014.
DOI: 10.1057/9781137449320.0011.

Davis and Sumara (1997) provide alternative conceptions of teaching and learning that stress complexity and a systems approach:

> That which we call "teaching" and that which we call "learning" might be better understood as mutually specifying, co-emergent, pervasive, and evolving practices that are at the core of our culture's efforts at self-organization and self-renewal. (p. 123)

To put this differently, we can think of teaching as the subsystem of society that generates the intelligence for the society to maintain itself. Thinking of teaching as generating *intelligence* requires a different conception of schooling than seeing teaching as producing compliance or uniformity. Intelligence is a function of diversity. Recall Dewey's conception of intelligence as the "capacity to estimate the possibilities of a situation and to act in accordance with [that] estimate" (LW 4.170). Having multiple perspectives increases the range of possibilities that can be imagined, and having diverse skills and abilities increases the likelihood that various possibilities can be realized.

The complexity of teaching

Above, we discussed the complexity of learning. Partly because learning is complex, teaching is complex as well. Theories that describe what happens at certain levels in a classroom (such as changes in an individual brain, or how group dynamics work) are incapable of describing the complexity of the whole classroom. In addition, applying insights from one discipline may work quite well in understanding some phenomena, but not others. Thus, to begin to understand the complexity of teaching requires a "transdisciplinary" approach (Jorg, Davis & Nickson, 2007).

Understanding the complexity of teaching requires paying attention not only to the teacher's unique individual complexities, but to the complexities of different teaching contexts, including the expectations that schools and society have for teachers, and the particular mix of personalities and prior experiences among the students in a classroom (Seltzer-Kelly et al., 2011). These contextual variations—and the interrelationships among all of the various aspects and systems involved—play a huge role in determining how a teacher teaches, and whether the teaching is successful (Santoro, 2011).

DOI: 10.1057/9781137449320.0011

What is teaching?

What is **teaching**? A classic definition is "*teaching* is the process by which one person interacts with another with the *intention* of influencing his learning" (Johnson, 1967, p. 137). Such a definition is too simplistic to capture the reality of most teaching situations.

What is the teacher trying to do? Is it "maintaining order among divided, discrete entities" (Minnich 2006, p. 155). This may be "the pedagogue's view of life," where

> ... plurality, the lively differences among students, is considered a problem. It is to be reduced to sameness. Activity, the expressed liveliness of physical and social beings experiencing the world in which they are naturally interested, is also considered a problem. It is to be reduced to stillness. All the generative energy is to come from the teacher; the students are to receive, to take in, to store, to replicate. (Minnich, 2006, p. 156)

Alternatively, teaching can be seen in terms of "how to connect with and enhance [students'] lively natural, social interests by helping them learn how to pursue them effectively" (p. 156). Such a view understands that teaching involves a back-and-forth with the students rather than simple *do this and that* commands. This requires "surveying the capacities and needs of the particular set of individuals" and teaching in a way that develops those capacities rather than another set (Dewey, *Experience and Education*, 1938, LW 13.36). Notice that Dewey draws attention to the capacities of a *set* of individuals. We'll return to this in a moment.

Good teachers create rich experiences for students that promote human flourishing (Stables, 2008). Because students (and classrooms) are unique, this function cannot be standardized or scripted.

> Such, we argue, is the principal role of the teacher: to orient the attentions of learners and, in the process, to assist in the exploration of the space of the existing possible, thus opening up spaces of the not-yet imaginable.... Teaching, like learning, is not about convergence onto a pre-established truth, but about divergence—about broadening what can be known and done. In other words, the emphasis is not on what *is*, but on what might be brought forth. Teaching thus comes to be a participation in a recursively elaborative process of opening up new spaces of possibility while exploring current spaces. (Davis & Sumara, 2007, p. 64)

This evokes an image of *collective* intelligence, arising among a set of students. Involving students in democratic decision-making about

DOI: 10.1057/9781137449320.0011

what goes on in the classroom may be a necessary condition of allowing collective intelligence to emerge, requiring teachers not to maintain central control so much as find a way to disperse control—to *distribute* leadership. This includes being flexible enough to respond to emerging student interest or suggestions.

To complexify things further, the entities that float around in the classroom and interact aren't just the students and the teacher; they are the ideas, methods, and questions generated. How the teacher responds to this complex mix of entities determines whether the students learn about the complexity of reality or just learn to fill out worksheets. If teachers conceive of their students as inquirers, they will be less likely to minimize student involvement in the educational situation, and to admit that students can be teachers too.

Teachers as inquirers

Just as *students* vary considerably from one another due to their families, genetics, and experiences, so too do teachers. Similarly, expecting teachers to comply—or to teach in the same way as everyone else (via a script or rigid curriculum)—causes disconnects. Rather than seeing the difference among teachers as a problem, it would be better to design the larger system to allow teachers flexibility so that their uniqueness can become a strength. Schools are *not factories*; there is no need for all teachers to be aiming at the same outcomes. As Dewey stresses throughout his work, it is *growth* that is wanted, not incremental development of highly specified knowledge or skills.

Teachers themselves are individuals, with unique potentials, and a teacher's unique potential isn't fully developed, no matter what stage she is in her career. Development does not end until a person's death. (If it does end before that, the person will fall into a lifeless routine.) Teachers also serve as *role models* in the development of their students' unique potentials, which qualifies their ongoing personal development as a *professional* obligation.

As schools move away from standardization and towards customization, teachers need to adopt new frameworks for paying attention in their classrooms. Seeing their classrooms as complex social systems—ecologies—is part of this shift (Seltzer-Kelly et al., 2011).

Dewey devoted considerable attention to the question of how teachers can improve their practice. He wanted teachers to develop intellectual methods and tools for deepening their understanding of classrooms and

DOI: 10.1057/9781137449320.0011

the effectiveness of their practices. He emphasized paying attention to *relations* in the classroom, and developing the ability to generalize from multiple experiences. He warned against trying to turn teaching into a set of recipes or procedures:

> Laws and facts, even when they are arrived at in genuinely scientific shape, do not yield *rules of practice*. Their value for educational practice—and *all education* is a mode of practice, intelligent or accidental and routine—is indirect; it consists in provision of *intellectual instrumentalities* to be used by the educator. (*The Sources of a Science of Education*, 1929, LW 5.14)

Dewey emphasized the complexity of teaching, making understanding it much more difficult than understanding in the hard sciences, where it is possible to exclude variables by controlling conditions:

> In educating individualities, no such exclusion can be had. The number of variables that enter is enormous. The intelligence of the teacher is dependent upon the extent in which he takes into account the variables that are not obviously involved in his immediate special task. Judgment in such matter is of qualitative situations and must itself be qualitative. (LW 5.33)

Teachers need to come to understand each student they encounter. This is enormously complex, involving openness to almost an infinite variety of persons. Qualitative uniqueness is a generic trait of *all* individuals.

Intersubjectivity

We become who we are through interaction with others. When we encounter another person, our habits are challenged. In responding to this challenge, we have an opportunity for growth.

Intersubjectivity can be defined as the space of shared experience with others, especially in the sense that the shared experience is experienced differently by each individual. Our awareness that another person is experiencing the same event as we are, but experiencing it differently than we are, is a *resource* for us to understand our own subjectivity but also to become aware of the possibility of increased objectivity. Intersubjectivity thus helps us to learn that the truth may be different than we ourselves see it. It therefore helps in developing empathy (and caring) and gives us an opportunity for growth (Sumara, Davis, & Iftody, 2008).[1]

The classroom is particularly important as a kind of laboratory for learning how to relate to others, since students inevitably encounter others who experience things differently than themselves; thus, it is also

DOI: 10.1057/9781137449320.0011

an ideal setting for learning morality. This moral aspect of teaching is fundamental to the profession (Santoro, 2011)—that is, if the school is structured in a way that allows this purpose to be fulfilled and if the teacher and students are willing to allow the emergence of real existential differences, rather than trying to avoid difference. A "discriminating mind" will "open itself up to contingent experiences (listening) by letting itself be irritated" (Lehmann-Rommel, 2000, p. 215). Teachers need to watch their desire—and that of their students—for "security and unambiguity" and their "impatience and distrust in open processes in the realization of pedagogical goals and values" (p. 216). This requires seeing the classroom not as a set of people who are complete in themselves, interacting about some piece of subject-matter, but as a space for dynamic interactions to occur: a space of intersubjectivity.

Increasingly, schools are structured in a way that limits this moral dimension. Pre-scripted curriculum, heavy-handed administrative oversight (often itself coming from policy makers above the administrators), and evaluations of teaching effectiveness based on student performance on standardized tests forces teachers to emphasize the technical and mechanical aspects of their job more than the interpersonal or intersubjective. This impoverishes the process of education and demoralizes teachers, many of whom have gone into the profession because of the possibility it offers of making a true difference in the lives of children. "What is called for is not the arrogance of institutionalized knowledge with its rigid standards, categories, and identities, but acknowledgement, respect, and, perhaps, recognition" (Garrison, 2003, p. 351).

Caring

To reiterate what was said above about the complexity of learning, we must always see it as an *interaction* between (at least) the learner and the teacher, which highlights the fact that learning is *always* about (at least one) relationship (Biesta, 2001). Nel Noddings' (2012) conception of caring as a dyad of the one cared for and the one caring—with a *relation* of care between them—provides a powerful, systems-based approach to thinking about relationships. It also provides guidance for educating caring people. As Noddings writes, "In care ethics, relation is ontologically basic, and the caring relation is ethically (morally) basic. Every human life starts in relation, and it is through relations that a human individual emerges" (p. 771). Notice the use of the words "relation" and "emerge."

DOI: 10.1057/9781137449320.0011

To care is to attend to the other, to listen to his expressed needs. Teachers who seek to exemplify the caring relation towards their students are therefore potentially faced with the dilemma of whether to put the child's needs ahead of the curriculum. They must be reflective about this decision, and must respond—not necessarily by putting the child's needs first, but in a way that "maintains the caring relation" (p. 772). This may include engaging in dialogue to better understand the expressed needs. The student's role is to respond to the caring in some way.

The educational goal of developing the capacity to care in students is furthered by increasing their capacity to be "moved" by the expressed needs of others: to empathize, not in an intellectual way, but in a *responsive* way.

It is hard for young people to care when others aren't really caring for them. Today's culture often excludes teenagers from participation and isolates them, using medications and harsh punishments to force conformity to seemingly arbitrary social expectations (Currie, 2005). Abbott and McTaggart (2010) refer to the lack of care for teenagers in our society as "shoulder-shrugging individualism" (p. 183; see also Hersch, 2013).

Teacher education

Teacher education, like schooling in general, but perhaps more so, is seen as largely ineffective by the American general public. This reflects the historical origins of teacher education outside of universities (in so-called normal schools), the view at many universities that colleges of education faculty are of a lower status than others in the academic community, and the fact that education majors tend to be the least-well prepared academically among all undergraduate majors (Levine, 2006). Teacher education candidates have come out of a system that has fairly conventional expectations of thinking, focusing on academic knowledge, analysis, and compliance rather than understanding complexity. These prior experiences "inform what they want to do and how they want to do it" (Boyles, 2006, p. 66).

Education classes, especially those focused on teaching methods, are considered "gut" classes at many universities. In the eyes of some, such classes are devoid of intellectual content, and seem unduly focused on "how to teach," often in a way that reflects the progressive philosophical

DOI: 10.1057/9781137449320.0011

views of teacher educators rather than the importance of subject matter or effective incorporation of what is known about the complexity of learning (Hirsch, 2006). Others lament the fact that "there is precious little consideration given to how children learn, to the philosophic questions that have to be answered in every generation as to why we think as we do" (Abbott & McTaggart, 2010, p. 179). Even some sympathetic commentators decry the way teachers are prepared to be heterogeneous do-it-yourselfers within loosely coupled systems, who often become conservative and habit-bound as their career progresses, with limited creativity and little use of theory or research (Hatton, 1988). Such criticism has led to increasing support for charter schools—which often do not require their teachers to be certified—and alternative pathways into teaching, such as Teach for America.

Of course, evaluations of the quality of teacher education are difficult if there is a lack of agreement of what good teaching is *for*. Many critics expect teachers to offer *consistent* and *even* results, such as in this *New York Times* op-ed:

> There is no widely agreed-upon knowledge base, training is brief or nonexistent, the criteria for passing licensing exams are much lower than in other fields, and there is little continuous professional guidance. It is not surprising, then, that researchers find wide variation in teaching skills across classrooms; in the absence of a system devoted to developing consistent expertise, we have teachers essentially winging it as they go along, with predictably uneven results. (Mehta, 2013, p. A21)

The question is: consistent expertise toward what ends? How are results measured? If what Mehta means is that teachers are inconsistent in raising scores on standardized tests (and there are few alternative measures of teaching effectiveness), then maybe what teachers are actually doing is developing diversity in a way that reflects some of the arguments I've made in this book.

The failure of teacher education as a field to demonstrate its effectiveness in preparing teachers is therefore in part a failure to convince the American public of what our schools are *for*. The truth is, teacher education is complex, involving the teacher's own experiences as a student and as a teacher candidate as well as the many challenges of learning to teach (Seltzer-Kelly et al., 2011). If part of what we want from teachers is to help diverse individuals develop their own unique potentials for excellence, then effective programs must include attention to the development of

DOI: 10.1057/9781137449320.0011

imagination and of understanding of the role of ideals in motivating growth (Cunningham, 2011).

Some programs of teacher education are widely praised. Graduate programs—which accept only teacher candidates who have undergraduate degrees in another field—tend to be of higher quality. The National Board of Professional Teaching Standards has developed National Board Certification for Teachers, which requires candidates to demonstrate reflectivity, strong command of subject-matter, and effective planning and assessment (Darling-Hammond, 2006). This program doesn't aim toward *consistency* or *evenness* using standardized assessments; rather, it incorporates highly developed sets of *criteria* for evaluating teaching performance. As I suggested above, using criteria instead of standards allows for diverse ways of demonstrating excellence rather than seeking to make all teachers do the same things in the same way. This type of approach is better suited to a diverse democratic society. But accepting it will require abandoning the idea that schooling should try to make teachers and students the same. Allowing differences in the ways that different teacher candidates handle the challenges they face, and facilitating learning among cohorts from those differences, fosters reflection in a way that trying to get everyone to handle things the same does not (Doll, 2011).

The transition from initial teacher certification to actual work in schools presents special difficulties. New teachers often find that the methods they have been taught in their methods classes are not widely used in schools and criticized directly by veteran teachers (Lesley, Gee & Matthews, 2010), and often the technological or other resources they were trained on are unavailable. In many schools, new teachers learn quickly from more veteran teachers that their job is more about cajoling students to accept school "knowledge" and expectations that it is to prepare them to live in a complex and changing world. Teachers need to be educated to expect *more* from their students—more, indeed, than was asked of themselves. This is without question a wicked problem.

Successful schooling requires teachers to serve as role models for students, both in terms of their academic habits and in terms of their attitudes. They also need well-developed social-emotional competence in order to support the complex mix of unique potentials in any classroom (Cunningham, 2011). This is a highly important function in society, yet we tend to take it lightly. As Noddings (2012) argues, teachers need an "unusually broad intellectual competence" (p. 777) and teacher

DOI: 10.1057/9781137449320.0011

education programs should somehow ensure this, rather than leaving subject-matter learning up to others.

Trusting teachers

Teachers increasingly do not feel respected or trusted (Santoro, 2011). Teachers respond to new expectations from school leaders (which are often passed down from the district level and beyond) by shuffling their own priorities. Inevitably, when new work is expected (for example, new paperwork, or new non-teaching responsibilities such as hall or lunchroom duty), this affects their primary work in classrooms. In one study of teaching, "Concern for the quality of their own work and the welfare of their students punctuated every conversation.... There is a growing sense of powerlessness that results from structures imposed from elsewhere over which the school has no control" (Fink, 2003, p. 19). A mid-career teacher stated, "I think teachers are less trusted now than they used to be. They're certainly not held in any sort of esteem and that's one of the things that I feel very strongly about. Now I'm just an instrument of the government and somehow I'm not doing a very good job" (p. 123). Another stated, "After a while, when people keep telling you 'you're bad, you're bad, you're bad,' eventually you start to believe it and you do start to take it personally and then it starts to spiral and you find yourself thinking 'maybe I am not doing a good job'" (p. 123).

If teacher education and professional development are of high quality, then teachers should be given the latitude to apply their professional judgment as needed in their own classrooms. "Good teachers must be allowed to use their professional and moral judgment in responding to the needs of their students" (Noddings, 2012, p. 774). This may include setting aside subject matter to build a trusting relationship with the student: one which motivates the student to attend to the curriculum.

In schools where teachers have been given increased autonomy and involvement in school-wide decision making, teachers often respond by individualizing learning, creating more active participation in learning activities for students, and finding ways to maximize the use of resources (Dirkswager, Farris-Berg & Junge, 2012; see also Levin, 2006). Increasing trust in general helps schools to better organize themselves around the tasks of instructional improvement (Bryk & Schneider, 2002; Tschannen-Moran, 2014).

DOI: 10.1057/9781137449320.0011

Note

1 Gert Biesta has suggested that we should speak of "transubjectivity" to emphasize that the space of understanding between people isn't between two already-constituted, self-sufficient subjects, but rather is a space in which the subjects themselves come to be, or are becoming (Vanderstraeten & Biesta, 2001, p. 19, n. 2; see also Zhao, 2012).

DOI: 10.1057/9781137449320.0011

7
The Schooling We Need

Abstract: *A variety of alternatives to standardization are offered, and specific suggestions are made for a curriculum for human flourishing in a democracy, including the need to personalize learning, adapt it to the twenty-first century, develop critical thinking, include attention to the arts, sustainability, and cosmopolitanism, and help students to understand the nature of nature and complexity and strive for wisdom.*

Cunningham, Craig A. *Systems Theory for Pragmatic Schooling: Toward Principles of Democratic Education.* New York: Palgrave Macmillan, 2014.
DOI: 10.1057/9781137449320.0012.

 DOI: 10.1057/9781137449320.0012

No single person can know everything, so what should we make sure that every person knows?

This is a tough question, because as I've been saying, we want to give individual students the freedom to pursue their own interests, and to allow teachers the autonomy to make day-to-day decisions about the activities and learning going on in their own classrooms. We also need to celebrate diversity and support teaching approaches that produce divergent outcomes.

The curriculum that schools have now is habituating our children to doing the same things they are doing now. This is a "betrayal of the creative potential of experimental intelligence" (Lehmann-Rommel, 2000, p. 202); it is dehumanizing. The only conception of learning that doesn't dehumanize students is an open-ended conception that allows them to pursue their interests in an environment that continually invites them to invent their own future. Without creating citizens with these desires and abilities, we are likely consigning our children to a difficult future of political gridlock, ever-increasing inequality, and a climate crisis that will get worse and worse.

Dewey writes:

> If one conceives that a social order different in quality and direction from the present is desirable and that schools should strive to educate with social change in view by producing individuals not complacent about what already exists, and equipped with desires and abilities to assist in transforming it, quite a different method and content is indicated. ("Progressive Education and the Science of Education," 1928, LW 3.362)

What is this "quite different" method and content?

Most importantly, the goals of schooling needs to be described in terms of criteria rather than standards. Criteria allow and encourage diversity. Standards represent a "lowest common denominator" that defines the least that is acceptable; criteria, on the other hand, allow for excellence to emerge.

Schooling is complex at *all* levels, but as we move from level to level, or system to system, we need to treat individual students and teachers as individuals, with their own unique potentials for excellence, and never to commodify them or treat them as mechanisms or reduce them to particular attributes or statistical variables. (*All statistical variables are gross simplifications!*) Each person is fundamentally irreducible to any one (or even a set of) their attributes, and each person deserves to be treated

DOI: 10.1057/9781137449320.0012

as immeasurably valuable and irredeemably unique. For schooling to take these principles into account, it has to change its aims, methods, structures, and systems. These seem fundamental to respecting the complexity of learning and teaching.

We have already defined in this book the basic principles that can guide the necessary changes. These are based on the concepts of unique potential and democracy. In short,

- Schooling should develop the unique potential of each individual and nurture and support diversity rather than trying to get people to conform to predefined academic standards.
- Schooling should give up the notion that compelling compliance is a necessary or even acceptable aspect of schooling. Schools are not prisons, or cattle ranches, or assembly lines. Schools do not exist for the convenience of administrators or teachers, or to enforce simplistic conceptions of what it means to be human.
- Schools ought to be arenas of experimentation in what it means to be human.

We need to reframe schools as *learning environments*, "bounded and structured [in a way] that allows for unlimited agency to build and experiment with things within those boundaries" (Thomas & Brown, 2011, p. 19).

Learning needs to be redefined as *growth*. This open-ended conception must replace the notion of "learning" as conformity with predefined objectives. Growth can, and should, be subject to assessment, but assessment based on criteria, rather than standards. As Ravitch (2010) wrote:

> When we define what matters in education only by what we can measure, we are in serious trouble. When that happens, we tend to forget that schools are responsible for shaping character, developing sound minds in healthy bodies and forming citizens for our democracy, not just for teaching basic skills. (p. 167)

Democracy and complexity

Stuart Kauffman (1995) stresses the ways that an understanding of complexity can help to justify diversity:

> The emerging sciences of complexity offer fresh support for the idea of a pluralistic democratic society, providing evidence that it is not merely a human

DOI: 10.1057/9781137449320.0012

> creation but part of the natural order of things.... Democracy has evolved as perhaps the optimal mechanism to achieve the best attainable compromises among conflicting practical, political, and moral interests. (p. 5)

What is it about democracy that makes it an "optimal mechanism" for handling complexity?

A democratic society is the ideal exemplar of distributed intelligence. Freedom and diversity foster more diversity. Diversity and difference are the engines of innovation. In a democracy, individuals are free to pursue their ends freely, to form groups based on shared interests, and to work with others to develop new ways of meeting the challenges they face, to differentiate themselves from others, to seek virtue, and to actualize their unique potential. People don't learn to live in a democratic way through autocratic structures of schooling. Schools themselves must become democratic.

Democracy is a way of selecting those innovations that will survive and thrive in the larger society. Instead of having a central authority decide "what works," democracy encourages diverse solutions. Those solutions that have general utility will spread; those solutions with only limited applicability will likely remain rare or will disappear completely. This is a natural selection of ideas, allowing the evolution of intelligence.

This provides a basic principle for educational policy: *Democracy works!*

There is no need for someone at the "top" of a social order to decide what approaches should be adopted everywhere. Indeed, such efforts at control stifle creativity and foster routine. These are not only the enemies of innovation, but are downright uninspiring for all.

Having good ideas selected naturally and organically allows for maximum overall flexibility and adaptability. A democratic system can control or self-organize *itself. Democracy is cybernetic. Thus democracy is the best way to organize complex adaptive systems—what above we referred to as* living synergistic social systems—*to produce learning and innovation and to realize diverse human purposes.*

The young people we need

The young people we need are intelligent, self-organizing, creative, determined, and aware of what's going on in the world. They are not clones of one another. They are not mirror images of their parents, of the norms of their community or larger society, or even of their own

DOI: 10.1057/9781137449320.0012

limited visions. They embrace expansive ideals, idealizing and seeking what they envision, while working towards virtue or excellence.

They seek to know themselves and to become who they are. They believe in themselves, are able to communicate and cooperate, are able to think for themselves, care for others, and understand the nature of reality. They do not think they know everything, but are open to learning more: to gaining wisdom.

How can schools be structured to facilitate this kind of individual?

One approach to develop stronger relations between teachers and their students (and with the students' parents or other caregivers) is to allow students to stay with the same teacher for more than one year—sometimes called "looping" (Noddings, 2012). Bringing teachers and parents into more intimate collaborative inquiry about the possibilities of particular students is going to help develop unique potential.

We should transform schools into purpose-driven learning organizations devoted to human flourishing.

A curriculum for human flourishing

William Doll reminds us that our current curriculum is atomistic and reductionistic. He advocates rethinking curriculum in terms of systems concepts such as interrelationships, emergence, networks, and patterns. Doing so would go far to eliminating the linear/factory notion of applying small bits of decontextualized and "equal" treatments to students at each stop on the assembly line. Doll (who admits to loving alliteration) promotes alternatives that are "recursive, relational, rigorous, and emerge from a curriculum rich in possibilities, problematics, perturbations" (2011, p. 35). He urges us to acquaint our students with wonder.

Twenty-first-century learning

Since at least the late 1950s, schools have been seen as tools for ensuring scientific, technological, and economic competitiveness. The time has come to rethink this.

"In the 21st century...recognition of our global interdependence and a commitment to cooperation must replace the 20th-century emphasis on competition" (Noddings, 2012, p. 777). In addition to these shifts in values, our curriculum also needs to shift to incorporate attention to systems thinking. This will require rethinking the school's relationship

DOI: 10.1057/9781137449320.0012

to the outside world, as Dewey urged; schools need to understand that there are resources available to provide the media and raw materials for exciting educational projects.

The next generation needs to have deeper learning about how interrelationships among systems produce complexity in local communities (including schools) and globally. Among the central concepts and skills are systems thinking, critical thinking, information literacy, adaptability, communication skills, appreciation of diversity, non-routine problem-solving, and modeling.

Murgatroyd (2010, p. 263) suggests reducing the amount of content in the curriculum, believing that "less is more" and that understanding is more important than coverage (Gardner, 2007). This approach gives more autonomy to teachers and allows for diversity in curriculum.

Some schools are incorporating *design* into the curriculum, having students solve real-world problems within constrained situations, requiring both creativity and rigor and requiring students to understand the role of compromise in designs. In school architecture, for example, designs that offer more natural light, shown to be conducive to learning, tend to be more expensive to heat. All design situations require compromise. For another example, as we saw above, additions to the curriculum always involve decisions about what to remove from the curriculum.

The need to balance conflicting interests is a fundamental problem not only of design but in nature: the designs that emerge from evolution always involve compromise, for example, the size of a baby's head at birth: if it were bigger, it couldn't fit between the mother's hip bones, but if it were smaller, it couldn't contain the amazing human brain (Kauffman, 1995; Mitchell, 2009). Given these multiple applications of design thinking, "design is a life skill" (Murgatroyd, 2010, p. 265). Design problems provide opportunities for student inquiry related to real-world "wicked" problems that require mastery of curriculum content as well as teamwork, creativity, and innovation. (In other words, they require embodied intelligence.)

Critical thinking/critical consciousness

If democracy "is to thrive from one generation to the next... the virtues of critical reason must be widely and deeply diffused among the citizenry" (Callan, 1994, p. 203). Callan lists some of the virtues of critical reason: "historical imagination, a capacity for discernment that is alert to ethical complexity and ambiguity, and competence in interpreting the

DOI: 10.1057/9781137449320.0012

bearing of the constitutive ideals of liberal democracy on the ongoing life of the polity" (p. 203).

What we *don't* want is to educate young people to be critical of our existing society to the point of abject cynicism or skeptical to the point of believing that ideals such as democracy are hopeless. Nor, as Callan (1994) reminds us, do we want a kind of reason that is completely dispassionate or claims to have risen above our particular perspectives. Instead, Callan urges that students learn an approach to history that includes what he calls "emotional generosity" and the use of imagination to find what is best in the historical traditions that we inherit. For example, the "self-evident" truths in the *Declaration of Independence* can become less compelling when young people learn that the author of that document himself owned slaves. But the principles themselves are still valuable. Surely we can agree that equality and liberty—as well as respect for difference—are essential to the American tradition despite our founders' failure to enact them.

We become conscious of our particular historical situation as we understand the problems we face. By understanding our particular life context, or situation, we come to understand the various systems of which we are a part. Understanding of the systems that impact on our lives is a critical awareness that leads to a critical consciousness: that is, a personal and experiential conscientious awareness of our own situation (Freire, 1970/2000). This is systems thinking at its core.

What we have to avoid is the tendency to see critical thinking in entirely instrumental terms. It's not a matter of just securing our self-interest through careful consideration of how we might manipulate the thinking of others by understanding their point of view. We have to consider the various political agendas that are operative in our larger society as well as the larger goals or purposes we serve (Bowers, 2012). I believe keeping democracy and the sacred value of each person's unique potential firmly in mind at all times is a useful corrective. As Dewey writes, "Education should create an interest in all persons in furthering the general good, so that they will find their own happiness realized in what they can do to improve the conditions of others" (Dewey, *Ethics*, 1932, LW 7.243).

The arts

An education in the arts "offers a powerful corrective to the prevailing modes of formal education today, with their limited—and experientially

DOI: 10.1057/9781137449320.0012

limiting—agenda of positivist fact gathering and behaviorist skill acquisition.... [and] nurtures...the native impulse to live life with an ever-expanding sense of meaning and value" (Granger, 2006, p. 3). A curriculum that includes the arts is more likely to develop capacities for creativity, self-expression, and divergent (or creative) thinking, and thus is going to be more effective in developing the unique potential of all students and not just those with linguistic or analytical strengths. Focusing on design, as mentioned above, helps bring the arts meaningfully into the curriculum in combination with science, technology, engineering, and math (STEM becomes STEAM), a way to avoid the marginalization of the arts that has occurred recently (Marshall, 2014). What's more, the arts help people to recognize patterns across multiple situations, a form of analogic thinking that is a fundamental component of thinking about systems.

Sustainability

Sustainability has to mean more than just staying in business. It must include a conception of human flourishing as well:

> A community worth sustaining would be alive—fresh, vital, evolving, diverse, dynamic. It would care about the quality as well as the continuation of life. It would recognize the need for social, economic, and environmental justice; and for physical, emotional, intellectual, cultural, and spiritual sustenance. (Stone, 2010, p. 34)

Education for sustainability involves active consideration of interrelationships throughout nature (Bowers, 2012). Stables (2007) describes understanding of ecology as a form of literacy, involving functional literacy (how to practice sustainability), cultural literacy (what natural resources do we as a society value), and critical literacy (which draws attention to ways to counteract purely economic decisions).

Joldersma (2009) argues that nature *needs* us to treat her differently. Given the complete dependence we have on nature, a central purpose of schooling ought to be helping students develop caring relations with nature, similar to those that Noddings suggests for interpersonal relations. Understanding the Earth as a living system, as suggested in the Gaia hypothesis, can help to develop this caring relation with nature. Even for urban students, we need creative ways to give direct experiences of the wonders of nature (Bowers, 2012). Without these interactions, people feel isolated from the natural environment, or begin to

DOI: 10.1057/9781137449320.0012

think that the human-made environment is what's real. Deepening our children's commitment to sustainability may be the only way our society can survive in anything like its current form.

Cosmopolitanism

With increasing globalization, there is a need for the development of ethical commitments that extend beyond one's own blood relatives or ethnic groups. Some have suggested that such commitments will be more universal (in terms of the diversity of people included in their principles) than any ethics based on a particular culture. The word "cosmopolitan" has been given to such systems, reflecting the idea that everyone (the entire cosmos) is included. The most articulate defender of the view that **cosmopolitanism** ought to replace the dictates of local culture is Martha Nussbaum (1994), who generated considerable controversy when she argued that schools ought to explicitly teach a common (or universal) cosmopolitan ethics to all students, worldwide, and ignore or downplay the significance of any more particularistic viewpoint.

A compelling argument for *balancing* this need for global consciousness with particular local concerns—even if those particular local concerns give preference to kinship or compatriots—was given by Appiah (2006), who suggests that people in a shrinking world need both a common cosmopolitanism *as well as* local commitments to particular others. Both forms of ethics develop, according to Appiah, from deep personal involvement with people of different cultures, *not* from any form of universal education. He would have educators avoid explicit attempts to develop cosmopolitan values, but instead wait for such values to emerge naturally through interactions across cultural boundaries.

By analogy, cosmopolitan values can be fostered through maintaining healthy cultural diversity in schools. Magnet schools or programs can increase diversity within schools. Teachers and administrators can encourage internal diversity by randomly assigning students to classes rather than using test scores, and can explicitly instruct students in how to listen to each other and to value divergent or innovative ideas. Some basic ethical rules can be established that prohibit bullying or the silencing of different points of view. Pedagogical methods can encourage students to think, rather than to just be what someone has decided they should be. As this shows, the construction of curriculum requires attention to more than just subject-matter. It may involve changes in school

DOI: 10.1057/9781137449320.0012

or district policies. Curriculum and policy are interpenetrating systems that need to co-evolve.

A curriculum on the nature of nature

As William Styron (1952) wrote in *Lie Down in Darkness*,

> Bunny, you can believe me, most kids these days are not wrong or wrongdoers, they're just aimless and lost, more aimless than you all ever thought of being.

This was quoted by Maxine Greene in 1957. Do we think *those* kids were lost? Today's kids live in a much more complex and confusing world, and rather than preparing them for it, we're preparing them for the world of the past. At what point are we going to be willing to say to them: "your future will be very different than our past, and so you need to learn to think in new ways"?

Many students leave schools with lots of random facts and skills but no understanding of systems in their complex contexts. As I have suggested, we can think of this missing piece as an understanding of the "nature of nature": of reality. Understanding the nature of nature requires a different type of learning.

Most people acquire their general sense of reality *outside* of school. This is not surprising. Schools contain rather artificial environments. There's generally not much that's similar to the real world in a school. Students graduate from school with no direct experience of many real world phenomena. They don't know how to fix electrical and mechanical devices, how things are designed or made, the nature of mental illness or how it's defined, the routines of doctors or lawyers or anyone else other than teachers, the actual workings of politics at the local or state level, the ways that data are used in scientific research, different philosophical ideas about knowledge or truth, or any deep knowledge of *any real* situations. Sure, there's some exposure to these things through textbooks and other readings, but that experience is *vicarious*, not direct or personal. And when students do *make* things in school or go on field trips or do experiments in science class, many of these experiences are so simplified from the real world versions as to be caricatures: "almost useless in practice" (Brown, Collins & Duguid, 1989, p. 32; Mashhadi & Woolnough, 1999). Acquiring *depth* is something that happens only with sustained interaction with a particular situation. If we don't dig deeply, we acquire shallow or superficial understanding.

DOI: 10.1057/9781137449320.0012

Some would say it's not the school's job to teach people about the real world, or the nature of nature. "*That's the parents' job.*" If most parents were wise enough to recognize that their children's interests and worlds often differ from their own, then this might make sense. Of course, parents aren't always available or qualified to teach these things.

The truth is that many young people are pretty much left on their own to piece together a good overall sense of reality. This is hard, given that we live "in a world without a stable center" (Garrison, 2003, p. 349)—a world, that is, in which there is little consensus about what matters and how best to think about how to structure a society committed to realizing a better future for all. Many kids manage to teach themselves quite a bit, given the tremendous amount of information available in books, movies, television, and online. Indeed, kids can, if they wish, learn more about any given topic on their own than they could ever learn in school (Cremin, 1990). However, because these out-of-school studies aren't typically systematic, kids might know a lot about a few subjects, or a little about a lot of subjects. Given this, combined with what they learn in school and through their home life, young people create what they take to be a coherent set of hypotheses about how things work (Hacker, 1994). But these worldviews are fragmentary. Most alarmingly, many young adults "have but a limited capacity to look beyond their restricted world-view to see the ecological, environmental, and social crises that are hurtling towards them" (Abbott & McTaggart, 2010, p. 7).

Students don't have to be *completely* in the dark about this comprehensive understanding of the way everything works. Once they get to college, academically successful students have the opportunity to participate in high quality synthetic experiences like freshman or senior seminars that provide scaffolding for an overall understanding of the nature of nature. Some students are able to gain a sense of the nature of nature through in-depth study of particular subjects, like literature, history, bioengineering, sociology, economics, or philosophy. Other people, who don't enroll in college, can gain understanding through reading books, if they are so inclined. Some of those books are philosophy books, although many of those are abstruse and inaccessible to the general public.

The world needs people who can think from multiple perspectives about complex situations. This requires overcoming the artificial boundaries our schools put up among different subjects or disciplines. Students need educational experiences with the interconnections of things.

DOI: 10.1057/9781137449320.0012

Recently issued standards statements suggest that there is a growing appreciation of the idea that over-arching concepts and general procedures are more important than isolated facts or skills (Marshall, 2014). For example, the Next Generation Science Standards include a set of "cross-cutting concepts": patterns; cause and effect; scale, proportion, and quantity; systems and system models; energy and matter; structure and function; and stability and change (NGSS Lead States, 2013). This bodes well for the hope that schools will embrace interdisciplinary approaches to thinking and learning.

Every student should—at least—have an opportunity to participate in an interdisciplinary seminar sometime between the ages of 13 and 18. The International Baccalaureate program provides a model in its Theory of Knowledge (TOK) core course:

> The fundamental question of TOK is "how do we know that?" Students are encouraged to think about how knowledge is arrived at in different disciplines, what the disciplines have in common and the differences between the disciplin[es].[1]

Focusing on epistemology is not the only way to organize such a synthetic experience. It could be organized around a broad topic such as "The Future" or "The Systems View of Life" (Capra & Luisi, 2014).

Students need to be able to think beyond disciplines, an approach Marshall (2014) refers to as "transdisciplinarity," which "rises above disciplines and dissolves their boundaries to create a new social and cognitive space" (p. 106), entailing "level-jumping across neurological, psychological, social, cultural, and other phenomena. One must be willing and able to think in terms of many nested systems, not some isolatable realm" (Davis 2005, p. 86). Fundamentally, students need to understand reality in terms of systems. This is a central component of wisdom.

Wisdom

How do standards incorporate wisdom? Most do not. This reflects their fundamentally reductionist orientation. But for our democracy to thrive, we need to cultivate wisdom in young people.

> The dictionary defines *wisdom* as judgment, discernment and insight (often a spiritual orientation), reason (traditional notion of learning and knowledge), common sense (often normative or values driven), understanding (often through empathy and relationships), and perception (through experience and observation). (Kezar, 2005, p. 50)

DOI: 10.1057/9781137449320.0012

Wisdom involves a willingness to move back and forth between particulars and the bigger picture. It requires a balance of analysis and synthesis: attention to distinctions *and* relations. It involves sensitivity, creativity, and a refusal to submit to an overly simplistic view of what it means to be human (Henderson, 2001). Wisdom, in short, is "a sense for the better kind of life to be led" (Dewey, "Philosophy and Democracy," 1919, MW 11.44).

We have two traditional ways of knowing in our culture: science and the humanities. Russell Ackoff suggests one way to distinguish these: "Science is the search for similarities among things that are apparently different, and the humanities are the search for differences among things that are apparently similar. Scientists seek the general and humanists seek the unique" (Ackoff, 1997, p. 433). It is the *synthesis* of these two approaches that results in the most effective approach to thinking complexly about complexity. It is also important not to forget evaluative thinking.

> A good education brings out the best in us by holistically unifying our character in knowledge, emotion, and action in service of desires directed toward the good—that is, those persons, things, and ideals that are deemed to be of most value. (Garrison, 1995, p. 409)

Thus, a good education is about passion and desire, not just thinking. Such an education will "allow us to invent new ways of being in our natural world, new ways of understanding, and new ways of interacting that celebrate and explore the interplay among matter and spirit, knowing and meaning, imagination and reality" (Fleener, 2005, p. 6).

Socrates tells us that the search for wisdom begins with humility. There is no way we can know how the world—and schooling—is going to change in the coming decades. But as Stuart Kauffman (1995) writes:

> All we can do is be locally wise, even though our own best efforts will ultimately create the conditions that lead to our transformations to utterly unforeseeable ways of being. We can only strut and fret our hour, yet this is our own and only role in the play. We ought, then, play it proudly but humbly. (p. 303)

Note

1 http://www.ibo.org/diploma/curriculum/

DOI: 10.1057/9781137449320.0012

Epilogue: Emergent Principles of Democratic Schooling

Abstract: *The book ends with a set of principles that emphasize the generic traits of existence, systems theory, complexity, diversity, unique potential, inquiry, and democracy. Together these principles offer a compelling vision of schools as communities contributing to democracy and human flourishing.*

Cunningham, Craig A. *Systems Theory for Pragmatic Schooling: Toward Principles of Democratic Education.* New York: Palgrave Macmillan, 2014.
DOI: 10.1057/9781137449320.0013.

Rather than looking to systems theory for *techniques* to improve schools, I have argued that we should use it to reframe the *meaning* and purpose of schooling, to reconstruct the effects that schooling has on our students.

The purpose of schooling in the 21st century must shift from disseminating knowledge, ensuring the competitiveness of the nation, and the sorting of students into a variety of well-defined career tracks to creating flourishing human beings and a better society.

Schools should be about bringing about an ideal future, not about doing things the way they have always been done, or about preparing students for today's (or yesterday's) world. School leaders—and everyone else involved in schooling—must be allowed to idealize and dream.

The primary lessons of this book can be stated rather simply as a set of principles:

- Systems theory—informed by pragmatic naturalism—focuses attention on interactions/transactions/interrelationships, complexity, qualitative uniqueness, and temporality, including the phenomenon of emergence.
- Paying attention to *both* distinctions *and* relations in understanding the systems involved in schooling helps avoid the perils of reductionism.
- The many systems of schooling—at all levels both within and outside of schools—are characterized by the qualities identified by Dewey as the generic traits: most importantly, interaction, temporality, complexity, and qualitative uniqueness.
- Schools need to be transformed from the factory model to becoming democratic spaces for the collaborative creation of shared meanings.
- Learning and teaching are complex, and the best approaches to both recognize diversity and encourage freedom and autonomy.
- To the extent that diversity and variation are encouraged, people and social systems become more powerful in effecting change.
- Curriculum standards should be made much less specific, and schools should be able to use alternative forms of assessment to demonstrate the learning of their students. Schools should develop their own *criteria* for assessment rather than relying on standards to foster diverse excellences.

DOI: 10.1057/9781137449320.0013

- School leaders should seek to liberate the creativity, imagination, and idealism of unique teachers and students and to build support for this approach among parents and community members.
- Students and teachers should learn to use transdisciplinary inquiry to respond to a complex world in ways that reflect their deepest ideals.
- A shared process of envisioning and working toward a better future for our schools, for our students, and for our society—involving wide democratic participation by diverse individuals—is energizing for everyone; it can even be fun!
- Schools should be sites of engagement, diversity, celebration, community, and joy.
- Democracy as an expansive social ideal motivates individual growth as well as a flourishing society.

For Dewey, democracy

> ...was the social ideal not only because it nurtured individual growth but because it envisioned a growing community that would itself be a complex, organic work of art, harmonizing "the development of each individual with the maintenance of a social state in which the activities of one will contribute to the good of all the others". (Westbrook, 1991, p. 416; quoting Dewey's *Ethics*, 1932, LW 7.350)

The phrase "complex, organic work of art" captures Dewey's religious devotion to democracy. As an ideal, it motivates individuals not only towards their own growth, but toward the formation of a better community.

> The democratic way of life is the embodiment of a spirit of sympathy, open communication, and cooperation joined together with experimentalism and imaginative vision, leading to freedom and ongoing growth for all. (Rockefeller, 1991, p. 444)

I invite you to realize this way of life in our schools and in the larger society.

DOI: 10.1057/9781137449320.0013

Bibliography

Abbott, J., & McTaggart, H. (2010). *Overschooled but undereducated: How the crisis in education is jeopardizing our adolescents*. London, UK: Continuum.

Ackoff, R. L. (1997). Systems, messes and interactive planning. *The Societal Engagement of Social Science, 3*, 417–438.

Anyon, J. (1997). *Ghetto schooling: A political economy of urban educational reform*. New York, NY: Teachers College Press.

Appiah, K.A. (2006). *Cosmopolitanism: Ethics in a world of strangers*. New York, NY: Norton.

Aristotle. (330 BC/1962). *Nicomachean ethics*. Martin Ostwald (Trans.). New York, NY: Macmillan.

Bánáthy, B. H. (1992). *A systems view of education*. Englewood Cliffs, NJ: Educational Technology Publications.

Bánáthy, B. H. (1995). Developing a systems view of education. *Educational Technology, 35*(3), 53–57.

Bánáthy, B. H. (1996). Information-based design of social systems. *Behavioral Science, 41*(2), 104–123.

Bánáthy, B. H. & Jenks, L. (1990). *The transformation of education by design: A leadership guide for educational decision makers*. San Francisco, CA: Far West Laboratory.

Barboza, D. (2010). Shanghai schools' approach pushes students to top of tests. *New York Times*, December 30, p. A4.

Barnard, P. A. (2013). *The systems thinking school: Redesigning schools from the inside-out*. Lanham, MD: Rowman & Littlefield.

DOI: 10.1057/9781137449320.0014

Bartos, J. (Ed.) (2012). *Do schools prepare students for a global economy?* Detroit, MI: Greenhaven Press.

Bassett, D. S., & Gazzaniga, M. S. (2011). Understanding complexity in the human brain. *Trends in Cognitive Sciences, 15*(5), 200–209.

Bateson, G. (2000/1972). *Steps to an ecology of mind.* Chicago, IL: University of Chicago Press.

Bateson, N. (2011). *An ecology of mind.* Oley, PA: Bullfrog Films.

Biesta, G. (2001). How difficult should education be? *Educational Theory, 51*, 385–400.

Biesta, G. (2007). Why "what works" won't work: Evidence-based practice and the democratic deficit in educational research. *Educational Theory, 57*(1), 1–22.

Boisvert, R. D. (1998a). *John Dewey: Rethinking our time.* Albany, N.Y: SUNY Press.

Boisvert, R. D. (1998b). Dewey's metaphysics: Ground-map of the prototypically real. In L. A. Hickman (Ed.), *Reading Dewey: Interpretations for a postmodern generation* (pp. 149–165). Bloomington: Indiana University Press.

Bonnett, M. (2009). Systemic wisdom, the "selving" of nature, and knowledge transformation: Education for the "greater whole." *Studies in Philosophy and Education, 28*(1), 39–49.

Bowers, C. A. (1985). Culture against itself: Nihilism as an element in recent educational thought. *American Journal of Education, 93*(4), 465–490.

Bowers, C. A. (2012). Questioning the idea of the individual as an autonomous moral agent. *Journal of Moral Education, 41*(3), 301–310.

Boyles, D. R. (2006). Dewey's epistemology: An argument for warranted assertions, knowing, and meaningful classroom practice. *Educational Theory, 56*(1), 57–68.

Bronfenbrenner, U. (1979). *The ecology of human development: Experiments by nature and design*. Cambridge, MA: Harvard University Press.

Bronfenbrenner, U. & Ceci, S. J. (1994). Nature-nurture reconceptualized in developmental perspective: A bioecological model. *Psychological Review, 101*(4), 568–586.

Brown, J. S., Collins, A., & Duguid, P. (1989). Situated cognition and the culture of learning. *Educational Researcher, 18*(1), 32–42.

Bryk. A. S. & Schneider, B. (2002). *Trust in schools: A core resource for improvement.* New York, NY: Russell Sage Foundation.

DOI: 10.1057/9781137449320.0014

Callan, E. (1994). Beyond sentimental civic education. *American Journal of Education, 102*(2), 190–221.

Capra, F., & Luisi, P. L. (2014). *The systems view of life: A unifying vision.* Cambridge, UK: Cambridge University Press.

Cohen, J. & Stewart, I. (1994). *The collapse of chaos: Discovering simplicity in a complex world.* New York, NY: Viking.

Coombs, P. H. (1968). *The world educational crisis: A systems analysis.* New York, NY: Oxford University Press.

Cremin, L. A. (1990). *Popular education and its discontents.* New York, NY: Harper & Row.

Cunningham, C. A. (1994). Unique potential: A metaphor for John Dewey's later conception of the self. *Educational Theory, 44*(2), 211–224.

Cunningham, C. A. (1995). Dewey's metaphysics and the self. *Studies in Philosophy and Education, 13,* 343–360.

Cunningham, C. A. (2011). Cultivating unique potential in schools: Revisioning democratic teacher education. In J. Kincheloe and R. Hewitt (Eds.), *Regenerating the philosophy of education: What happened to soul?* New York, NY: Peter Lang.

Currie, E. (2005). *Road to whatever: Middle-class culture and the crisis of adolescence.* New York, NY: Henry Holt.

Darling-Hammond, L. (2006). *Powerful teacher education: Lessons from exemplary programs.* San Francisco, CA: Jossey-Bass.

Davis, B. (2005). Teacher as consciousness of the collective. *Complicity: An International Journal of Complexity and Education,* 2(1), 85–88.

Davis, B. & Phelps, R. (2004). Complicity: An introduction and a welcome. *Complicity, 1*(1), 1–7.

Davis, B. & Simmt, E. (2003). Understanding learning systems: Mathematics education and complexity science. *Journal for Research in Mathematics Education, 34*(2), 137–167.

Davis, B. & Sumara, D. (1997). Cognition, complexity, and teacher education. *Harvard Educational Review, 67*(1), 105–126.

Davis, B. & Sumara, D. (2000). Another queer theory: Reading complexity theory as a moral and ethical imperative. *Thinking Queer: Sexuality, Culture, and Education,* 105–129.

Davis, B. & Sumara, D. (2007). Complexity science and education: Reconceptualizing the teacher's role in learning. *Interchange, 37*(1), 53–67.

Davis, B. & Sumara, D. (2008). Complexity as a theory of education. *TCI: Transnational Curriculum Inquiry,* 5(2), 33–44.

DOI: 10.1057/9781137449320.0014

Davis, B. & Sumara, D. (2010). "If things were simple...": Complexity in education. *Journal of Evaluation in Clinical Practice, 16*(4), 856–860.

Davis, B., Sumara, D. & Kieren, T. (1996). Cognition, co-emergence, curriculum. *Journal of Curriculum Studies, 28*(2), 151–169.

Dewey, J. (1969–1991). *The collected works*, In J. Boydston (Ed.), 37 vols. Carbondale: Southern Illinois University Press.

Dirkswager, E. J., Farris-Berg, K., & Junge, A. (2012). *Trusting teachers with school success: What happens when teachers call the shots.* Lanham, MD: R & L Education.

Doll, W. E. (2011). Response to Seltzer-Kelly, Cinnamon, Cunningham, Gurland, Jones & Toth. *Complicity 8*(1), 32–37.

Donald, M. (2001). *A mind so rare: The evolution of human consciousness.* New York, NY: Norton.

Dörner, D. (1997). *The logic of failure: Recognizing and avoiding error in complex situations.* Reading, MA: Addison-Wesley Pub.

Edelfelt, R. A. (1979). Schools as social systems. *Theory into Practice, 18*(5), 363–365.

Eisner, E. W. (1995). Standards for American schools: Help or hindrance? *Phi Delta Kappan, 76*(10), 758–760, 762–764.

Fink, D. (2003). The law of unintended consequences: The "real" cost of top-down reform. *Journal of Educational Change, 4*(2), 105–128.

Fleener, M. J. (2005). Chaos, complexity, curriculum and culture: Setting up the conversation. In W. Doll, M.J. Fleener, D. Truett & J. Julien (Eds.), *Chaos, complexity, curriculum, and culture* (pp. 1–17). New York, NY: Peter Lang.

Freire, P. (1970/2000). *Pedagogy of the oppressed.* New York, NY: Continuum.

Galinsky, E. (2010). *Mind in the making: The seven essential life skills every child needs.* New York, NY: HarperStudio.

Gardner, H. (1999). *Intelligence reframed: Multiple intelligences for the 21st century.* New York, NY: Basic Books.

Gardner, H. (2007). *Five minds for the future.* Boston, MA: Harvard Business School Press.

Garrison, J. (1995). Deweyan prophetic pragmatism, poetry, and the education of eros. *American Journal of Education, 103*(4), 406–431.

Garrison, J. (2003). Dewey, Derrida, and "the double bind." *Educational Philosophy & Theory, 35*(3), 349–362.

Godfrey-Smith, P. (1998). *Complexity and the function of mind in nature.* Cambridge, UK: Cambridge University Press.

DOI: 10.1057/9781137449320.0014

Gough, N. (1989). From epistemology to ecopolitics: Renewing a paradigm for curriculum. *Journal of Curriculum Studies, 21*(3), 225–241.

Granger, D. A. (2006). *John Dewey, Robert Pirsig, and the art of living: Revisioning aesthetic education*. New York, NY: Palgrave Macmillan.

Greenberg, G. (2004). The digital convergence: Extending the portfolio model. *Educause Review, 39*(4), 28–37.

Greene, M. (1957). The uses of literature. *Educational Theory, 7*(2), 143–149.

Hacker, D. J. (1994). An existential view of adolescence. *Journal of Early Adolescence, 14*, 300–327.

Hardin, G. (1968). The tragedy of the commons. *Science, 162*, 38–59, 1243–1248.

Hatton, E. (1988). Teachers' work as bricolage: Implications for teacher education. *British Journal of Sociology of Education, 9*(3), 337–357.

Henderson, J. G. (2001). Deepening democratic curriculum work. *Educational Researcher, 30*(9), 18–21.

Hersch, P. (2013). *A tribe apart: A journey into the heart of american adolescence*. New York, NY: Ballantine Books.

Hirsch, E. D. (1996). *The schools we need: And why we don't have them*. New York, NY: Doubleday.

Hirsch, E. D. (2006). Adequacy beyond dollars: the productive use of school time. In E. A. Hanushek (Ed.), *Courting failure: How school finance lawsuits exploit judges' good intentions and harm our children* (pp. 313–328). Stanford, CA: Education Next Books.

Hogan, D. M., & Tudge, J. R. H. (1999). Implications of Vygotsky's theory for peer learning. In A. M. O'Donnell & A. King (Eds.), *Cognitive perspectives on peer learning*, pp. 39–65. Mahwah, NJ: Lawrence Erlbaum Associates.

Hutchins, E. (2010). Cognitive ecology. *Topics in Cognitive Science, 2*(4), 705–715.

Jackson, P. W. (2002). *John Dewey and the philosopher's task*. New York, NY: Teachers College Press.

Jacoby, S. (2008). *The age of American unreason*. New York, NY: Pantheon Books.

James, W. (1890). *The principles of psychology*. New York, NY: Henry Holt and Co.

James, W. (1909/1971). *Essays in radical empiricism and a pluralistic universe*. New York, NY: Dutton.

DOI: 10.1057/9781137449320.0014

Jensen, E. (2008). *Brain-based learning: The new paradigm of teaching.* Thousand Oaks, CA: Corwin Press.

Johnson, M. (1967). Definitions and models in curriculum theory. *Educational Theory, 17*(2), 127–140.

Joldersma, C. W. (2009). How can science help us care for nature? Hermeneutics, fragility, and responsibility for the Earth. *Educational Theory, 59*(4), 465–483.

Jorg, T., Davis, B., & Nickmans, G. (2007). Towards a new, complexity science of learning and education. *Educational Research Review, 2*(2), 145–156.

Kauffman, S. A. (1995). *At home in the universe: The search for laws of self-organization and complexity.* New York, NY: Oxford University Press.

Kezar, A. (2005). What do we mean by "learning" in the context of higher education? *New Directions for Higher Education, 131*, 49–59.

Kitcher, P. (2011). Philosophy inside out. *Metaphilosophy, 42*(3), 248–260.

Kozlowska, K., & Hanney, L. (2002). The network perspective: An integration of attachment and family systems theories. *Family Process, 41*(3), 285–312.

Kyritsis, N., Kizil, C., & Brand, M. (2014). Neuroinflammation and central nervous system regeneration in vertebrates. *Trends in Cell Biology, 24*(2), 128–135.

Lauder, H., Young, M., Daniels, H., Balarin, M., & J. Lowe. (Eds). (2012). *Educating for the knowledge economy: Critical perspectives.* London, UK: Routledge.

Lehmann-Rommel, R. (2000). The renewal of Dewey—Trends in the nineties. *Studies in Philosophy & Education, 19*(1/2), 187–218.

Lesley, M., Gee, D., & Matthews, M. (2010). Separating the chaff of bureaucracy from the grain of pedagogy: Creating quality new teachers in the age of accountability. *Teacher Education Quarterly, 37*(2), 33–51.

Levin, B. B., & Schrum, L. (2013). Using systems thinking to leverage technology for school improvement. *Education, 46*(1), 29–52.

Levin, H. M. (2006). Worker democracy and worker productivity. *Social Justice Research, 19*(1), 109–121.

Levine, A. (2006). *Educating school teachers.* Washington, DC: The Education Schools Project.

MacLellan, Effie (1999). Reflective commentaries: What do they say about learning? *Educational Action Research, Volume 7*(3), 433–449.

DOI: 10.1057/9781137449320.0014

Marshall, J. (2014). Transdisciplinarity and art integration: Toward a new understanding of art-based learning across the curriculum. *Studies in Art Education, 55*(2), 104–127.

Mashhadi, A., & Woolnough, B. (1999). Insights into students' understanding of quantum physics: Visualizing quantum entities. *European Journal of Physics, 20*(6), 511.

Meadows, D. H., & Wright, D. (2008). *Thinking in systems: A primer.* White River Junction, VT: Chelsea Green Pub.

Mehta, J. (2013). Teachers: Will we ever learn? *New York Times*, April 13, p. A21.

Minnich, E. (2006). Dewey's philosophy of life. In D. Hansen (Ed.), *John Dewey and our educational prospect* (pp. 147–164). Albany, NY: State University of New York Press.

Mitchell, M. (2009). *Complexity: A guided tour.* Oxford, UK: Oxford University Press.

Muir, J. (1911/1990). *My first summer in the Sierra*. San Francisco: Sierra Club Books.

Murgatroyd, S. (2010). "Wicked problems" and the work of the school. *European Journal of Education, 45*(2), 259–279.

Nicolis, G. and Prigogine, I. (1977). *Self-organization in nonequilibrium systems: From dissipative structures to order through fluctuations*. New York, NY: John Wiley.

NGSS Lead States. (2013). *Next generation science standards: For states, by states*. Washington, DC: National Academies Press.

Noddings, N. (1988). An ethic of caring and its implications for instructional arrangements. *American Journal of Education 96*(2), 215–230.

Noddings, N. (2012). The caring relation in teaching. *Oxford Review of Education, 38*(6), 771–781.

Nordin, A. (2014). Crisis as a discursive legitimation strategy in educational reforms: A critical policy analysis. *Education Inquiry, 5*(1), 109–126.

Norton, D. L. (1976). *Personal destinies: A philosophy of ethical individualism*. Princeton, NJ: Princeton University Press.

Nussbaum, M. (1994). Patriotism and cosmopolitanism, *Boston Review, 19*(5).

Page, S. (2010). *Diversity and complexity*. Princeton, NJ: Princeton University Press.

DOI: 10.1057/9781137449320.0014

Pallant, A., Lee, H., & Pryputniewicz, S. (2012). Modeling Earth's climate. *Science Teacher, 79*(7), 38–42.

Pellegrino, J. W. & Hilton, M. L. (2012). *Education for life and work: Developing transferable knowledge and skills in the 21st century.* Washington, DC: The National Academies Press.

Putnam, H. (2002). *The collapse of the fact/value dichotomy and other essays.* Cambridge, MA: Harvard University Press.

Ravitch, D. (2010). *The death and life of the great American school system: How testing and choice are undermining education.* New York, NY: Basic Books.

Reigeluth, C.M. (2004). Educational systems design. In A. Kovalchik & K. Dawson (Eds.), *Education and technology: An encyclopedia.* Santa Barbara, CA: ABC-Clio.

Robinson, K. (2011). *Out of our minds: Learning to be creative.* Oxford, UK: Capstone.

Rockefeller, S. C. (1991). *John Dewey: Religious faith and democratic humanism.* New York, NY: Columbia University Press.

Ryder, J. (2013). *The things in heaven and earth: An essay in pragmatic naturalism.* New York, NY: Fordham University Press.

Santoro, D. A. (2011). Good teaching in difficult times: Demoralization in the pursuit of good work. *American Journal of Education, 118*(1), 1–23.

Scheffler, Israel. (1985). *Of human potential.* Boston, MA: Routledge.

Schulkin, J. (2012). *Naturalism and pragmatism.* Basingstoke, UK: Palgrave Macmillan.

Seltzer-Kelly, D. L., Cinnamon, S., Cunningham, C. A., Gurland, S. T., Jones, K., & Toth, S. (2011). (Re)imagining teacher preparation for conjoint democratic inquiry in complex classroom ecologies. *Complicity: An International Journal of Complexity & Education, 8*(1), 5–27.

Senge, P. M. (1990/2006). *The fifth discipline: The art and practice of the learning organization.* New York, NY: Doubleday/Currency.

Siegrist, G., Green, R., Brockmeier, L., Tsemunhu, R. & Pate, J. (2013). A brief history: The impact of systems thinking on the organization of schools. *National Forum of Educational Administration & Supervision Journal, 31*(4), 1–9.

Sizer, T. R. (1984). *Horace's compromise: The dilemma of the American high school: The first report from a study of high schools.* Boston, MA: Houghton Mifflin.

DOI: 10.1057/9781137449320.0014

Sizer, T. R. (1992). *Horace's school: Redesigning the American high school*. Boston, MA: Houghton Mifflin.
Skaburskis, A. (2008). The origin of "wicked problems." *Planning Theory & Practice*, 9(2), 277–280.
Smith, G., & Rabin, C. (2013). Modern education: A tragedy of the commons. *Journal of Curriculum Studies*, 45(6), 748–767.
Spillane, J.P. (2006). *Distributed leadership*. San Francisco, CA: Jossey-Bass.
Squire, K. D., & Reigeluth, C. M. (2000). The many faces of systemic change. *Educational Horizons*, *78*(3), 143–152.
Stables, A. (2007). Is nature immaterial? The possibilities for environmental education without an environment. *Canadian Journal of Environmental Education*, *12*(1), 55–67.
Stables, A. (2008). Semiosis, Dewey and difference: Implications for pragmatic philosophy of education. *Contemporary Pragmatism*, 5(1), 147–161.
Steg, D. R. (1996). Cybernetics. In J. J. Chambliss (Ed.), *Philosophy of education: An encyclopedia* (pp. 126–131). New York, NY: Garland Pub.
Stewart, C., Raskin, C., & Zielaski, D. (2012). Barriers to district-level educational reform: A statewide study of Minnesota school superintendents. *International Journal of Educational Leadership Preparation*, *7*(3).
Stone, M. K. (2010). A schooling for sustainability framework. *Teacher Education Quarterly*, *37*(4), 33–46.
Sumara, D., Davis, B., & Iftody, T. (2008). Educating for ethical know-how: Curriculum in a culture of participation and complicity. *Curriculum Matters*, 4, 20–39.
Taylor, C. (1989). *Sources of the self: The making of the modern identity*. Cambridge, MA: Harvard University Press.
Thomas, D., & Brown, J. S. (2011). *A new culture of learning: Cultivating the imagination for a world of constant change*. Lexington, KY: CreateSpace.
Tozer, S., Senese, G. B., & Violas, P. C. (2013). *School and society: Historical and contemporary perspectives*. New York, NY: McGraw-Hill.
Tschannen-Moran, M. (2014). *Trust matters: Leadership for successful schools*. New York, NY: John Wiley & Sons.
Tyack, David. (1991). Public school reform: Policy talk and institutional practice. *American Journal of Education*, *100*(1), 1–19.
United States. (1983). *A nation at risk: The imperative for educational reform*. Washington, DC: National Commission on Excellence in Education.

DOI: 10.1057/9781137449320.0014

Varela, F. J., Thompson, E., & Rosch, E. (1991). *The embodied mind: Cognitive science and human experience.* Cambridge, MA: MIT Press.

Vanderstraeten, R. (2000). Luhmann on socialization and education. *Educational Theory, 50*(1), 1–23.

Vanderstraeten, R. (2002). Parsons, Luhmann and the theorem of double contingency. *Journal of Classical Sociology, 2*(1), 77–92.

Vanderstraeten, R., & Biesta, G. (2001). How is education possible? Preliminary investigations for a theory of education. *Educational Philosophy and Theory, 33*(1), 7–21.

Waddock, S. A. (1998). Educating holistic professionals in a world of wicked problems. *Applied Developmental Science, 2*(1), 40–47.

Waks, L. J. (2014). *Education 2.0: The learning web revolution and the transformation of the school.* Boulder, CO: Paradigm Publishers.

Watson, K., Handala, B., Maher, M., & McGinty, E. (2013). Globalising the class size debate: Myths and realities. *Journal of International and Comparative Education, 2*(2), 72–85.

Weber, E. P., & Khademian, A. M. (2008). Wicked problems, knowledge challenges, and collaborative capacity builders in network settings. *Public Administration Review, 68*(2), 334–349.

Westbrook, R. B. (1991). *John Dewey and American democracy.* Ithaca, NY: Cornell University Press.

Whitehead, A. N. (1920). *The concept of nature: Tarner lectures delivered in Trinity college, November, 1919.* Cambridge, UK: The University Press.

Wiener, N. (1950). *The human use of human beings: Cybernetics and society.* New York, NY: Houghton Mifflin.

Wiggins, G. P., & McTighe, J. (2005). *Understanding by design.* Alexandria, VA: Association for Supervision and Curriculum Development.

Wilkinson, R. G., & Pickett, K. (2010). *The spirit level: Why greater equality makes societies stronger.* New York, NY: Bloomsbury Press.

Williams, B., & Hummelbrunner, R. (2011). *Systems concepts in action: A practitioner's toolkit.* Stanford, CA: Stanford Business Books.

Zhao, G. (2012). Levinas and the mission of education. *Educational Theory, 62*(6), 659–675.

DOI: 10.1057/9781137449320.0014

Index

DOI: 10.1057/9781137449320.0014

DOI: 10.1057/9781137449320.0014

DOI: 10.1057/9781137449320.0014

DOI: 10.1057/9781137449320.0014

DOI: 10.1057/9781137449320.0014

DOI: 10.1057/9781137449320.0014

DOI: 10.1057/9781137449320.0014

CPSIA information can be obtained at www.ICGtesting.com
Printed in the USA
LVOW07*1920271114

415877LV00001B/3/P